DEATH

What will

Hubert J. Richards was born in 1921. He studied in Rome, where he took degrees in theology and in scripture. From 1949 to 1965 he taught at St Edmund's College, Ware. In 1965 he was appointed principal of Corpus Christi College in London, an international institute of religious education. He retired from this post in 1972, and is now a lecturer in religious studies in the school of Education of the University of East Anglia.

He is widely known, both in England and abroad, as a lecturer on the problems of religious education, and as composer of a variety of gospel songs. He is author of: *God Speaks to Us, Christ In Our World* (with Peter De Rosa), *What The Spirit Says to the Churches, An ABC of the Bible, Forty Gospel Songs, Ten Gospel Songs, The Heart of a Rose, St Paul and his Epistles, What Happens When You Pray?, Pilgrim to the Holy Land, The Gospel in Song.*

DEATH
AND AFTER:
What Will Really Happen?

Hubert J. Richards

MOWBRAY
LONDON & OXFORD

ISBN 0 264 67103 1

This revised edition published 1986
by A. R. Mowbray & Co. Ltd,
Saint Thomas House, Becket Street,
Oxford, OX1 1SJ
First published in Great Britain
by Fount Paperbacks, London, 1980.

British Library Cataloguing in Publication Data

Richards, Hubert J.
    Death and after: what will really happen?
    — (Mowbrays popular christian paperbacks)
    1. Future life
    I. Title
    236'.2   BT902
    ISBN 0–264–67103–1

Typeset by Cotswold Typesetting Ltd, Cheltenham
Printed in Great Britain by Cox & Wyman Ltd, Reading

Dedicated to
the many discussion groups
whose members urged me
to put down these thoughts
of theirs and mine

ACKNOWLEDGEMENTS

Except where otherwise stated, scriptural quotations are taken from *The New Jerusalem Bible* (copyright © 1985 by Darton, Longman and Todd Ltd and Doubleday and Company Inc. Used by permission of the publishers). On a few occasions the author has felt free to make minor changes for the sake of precision.

Contents

1. Introduction

The story is told of the man who finally made it to the gates of Paradise, only to discover, to his surprise, that there were two entrances, not one. The notice on the first said, 'Heaven', on the second, 'Discussion on Heaven'. And this was the one everyone was queuing up for.

I have often used the story as a cautionary tale in discussion groups. We can get so engrossed in talking about something that we almost make it into a substitute for enjoying the real thing. To fall in love with the idea of love is not the same thing as loving. Some people are so full of the idea of community, and seize every opportunity to tell you so, that you could never bear to live with them. Community is about living with people, not talking about it. Loving is about loving people, not fantasizing about it. Heaven is about being at one with God, not discussing it.

THE QUESTIONING CHRISTIAN

The caution having been noted, it is none the less a fact that in recent years the topic of the 'hereafter' – death, judgement, resurrection, the afterlife, heaven, hell, etc.– has aroused an interest which it has not enjoyed for centuries. Judging from the discussion groups I have led, I do not see this simply as a vogue, a jumping on to the bandwagon of current fads, a flirtation with the occult in protest against the exaggerated materialism of our western society. It goes deeper. It has to do with the seriousness with which today's Christians are prepared to question things which their forefathers were content to accept as a simple matter of obedience, in the days when things were so because they had been taught they were so.

Modern Christians do not put such a premium on obedience. They are not only prepared to question things; they insist that it is their God-given duty to do so. 'Mother Church' notwithstanding, they will not be treated as children. For them, life is no longer seen as neatly mapped out for them by 'the authorities', with all the important decisions already made for them. Life is to be painfully worked out, with each situation offering a fresh challenge, a fresh invitation to look critically at inherited beliefs. What exactly do they mean? Can Christians still in honesty subscribe to them? To what precisely does their Christianity commit them?

For Christians of today, nothing is fixed and final. There are no questions which they regard as having been settled once and for all, not even the ultimate ones. Perhaps these least of all.

UNCHRISTIAN OTHERWORLDLINESS

There is a deeper reason still why contemporary Christians want to question the traditional beliefs about the 'hereafter'. As Christians, they are embarrassed by them.

For their Christianity has given them a profound sense of the sacredness of the world in which they live, and this is simply not compatible with the flight from the world implicit in the traditional teaching about death and eternal life. A preoccupation with the 'next' life effectively devalues the present one. If people think that their real treasure is in another world, they will be indifferent to the injustices of this world. Life becomes simply a vale of tears, a testing place, a pilgrimage which has no value of its own because it is only a preparation for journey's end. Life in this world can only be grudgingly tolerated. There is no point in trying to change it. Why bother to change earthly pounds into earthly dollars when the only currency you will eventually require is a heavenly one?

Auberon Waugh, interviewed by *The Times* in 1985, said (hopefully with tongue in cheek):

'You needn't worry about life on earth – social problems and so on – because we're only here for a short time and then there is eternity. It's not an admirable or particularly honest attitude but it's a fairly sane one.

I mean, I think it may be perfectly honourable to believe that the poor are hard done by, and that people are starving to death in Liverpool because they only get meat twice a week. But if you have this fallback position you can say, Well, people can live a perfectly good life on earth on meat twice a week. You can, of course, get worked up about it if you meet someone who is the object of injustice, but I think living in Somerset and worrying about Nicaragua is a sign of insanity.'

A religion expressed in these terms has little in common with the passionate social concern of the Old Testament prophets, or the preaching of Jesus of Nazareth. Freud called it a religion for infants, and Marx a drug, which serves the useful purpose of numbing the pain of the world men live in, but also

11

effectively paralyses them. Those who have come out of the anaesthetic have nothing but contempt for such a religion. They find it despicable, if not positively immoral, to encourage virtue by promises of future reward, and discourage vice by threats of punishment. A heaven which is no more than a carrot and a hell which is no more than a stick cannot be taken seriously. Nor can human life be taken seriously by those who adopt such an escapist philosophy.

If this is the case, perhaps one ought to give the Christian teaching about death a decent Christian burial. That is one option, and many have taken it. For them belief in an afterlife has gone dead, and they want nothing more to do with it.

But that is not the only option open to people. They could, for instance, ask what precisely the traditional language about death, judgement, hell and heaven is supposed to mean. Taking it seriously is not the same thing as taking it literally. How literally is it supposed to be taken?

What most people have found objectionable, or suspect, or at least unintelligible about this traditional language, is its literal interpretation. Is this literalness part of the Christian message, or a distortion of it? True enough, preachers have insisted heavily on a literal 'everlasting life' awarded to the virtuous in a literal 'heaven' literally 'after' death, and offered it for acceptance to the faithful under pain of literal 'hell-fire'. But is this the only way in which the New Testament data on the topic can be understood? Is it even possible that traditional Christian preaching has misinterpreted the Gospel?

It is an axiom in theology that God is so far beyond our comprehension that language about him can never be literal, only metaphorical. What we say about God can never be more than approximative, and therefore inadequate. The symbols and images we use to say something about God may serve up to a point, but beyond that they may be so unsatisfactory that they can be positively misleading. St Thomas Aquinas shrewdly observed that any statement about God, however true, will be less true than its opposite (See *Summa Contra Gentiles* 1, 30).

This is not always appreciated by those who listen to or read what theologians have to say: it too is metaphorical and inadequate. But then, to be fair, theologians themselves have not always accepted the in-built limitations of their God-talk. In their enthusiasm they can give the impression – and perhaps themselves half believe – that they know God like the back of their hands. But the God who can be spoken of with such glib assurance simply is not God. Those who talk of God must begin with the axiom that they don't know what they are talking about. And this is true not only of 'popular' theologians, and 'modern' theologians, but also of 'official' theologians, and of the great 'classical' theologians, and of those who have formulated 'Church doctrine', and of the biblical writers themselves.

If by definition, then, talk about God and our relationship with him can only be tentative and halting, what shall we say about talk on the afterlife? This is surely the darkest area of our understanding of God, where dogmatic statements would be even more out of place than anywhere else.

About some aspects of our relationship with God we

can at least speak from what we have ourselves experienced, from what our lives have taught us to be the case. But on this aspect there is no experience to appeal to. Our experience is limited to what lies this side of our death. What, if anything, lies on the other side, can be experienced only by those who have undergone death, and they are not telling.[1]

EYE HATH NOT SEEN

We have no experience, our own or anyone else's, of what lies beyond death. This means that there is no information to be had, and no one ought to speak as if there was. If we are to talk on the matter at all, we have no right to give the impression that we are describing things that have actually been seen, heard and handled. Theology books which read like a Blue Guide to the 'other world' should be prosecuted for fraud. True enough, they all preface their treatise with the famous disclaimer:

> Eye hath not seen, nor ear heard,
> Neither hath it entered into the heart of man
> What things God hath prepared
> For them that love him. (1 Corinthians 2.9)

But far from being deterred by the saying, they merrily proceed to describe what God hath prepared in precise detail, and offer maps and planned tours as if their eye at least had been granted a privileged preview.

[1] I do not deal, here, with the evidence of those who recover from apparent death, or of those who claim to have had contact with the 'spirits' of the departed. Even where this evidence is taken seriously, the alleged revelations are too trivial to count as hard information.

There is no information about the 'next' world. The only world we have information about is the world of which we have present experience.

Does this mean that all we can do about the afterlife is keep silent? Perhaps. Certainly a reverent agnosticism is a more worthy response to the mystery of death than the glib assumption that there is no mystery in the matter at all. Confucius was humble enough to admit: 'We don't yet know about life; how can we know about death?'

Yet perhaps our present experience gives us sufficient grounds for making some valid inference about the future. Certainly St Paul thought so. In the text just quoted he is, paradoxically enough, saying the very opposite of what he is normally taken to mean. The context makes this clear. For the short poem is itself a quotation from the book of Isaiah, and Paul is contrasting that Old Testament ignorance of the future with the knowledge that has been made available in Christ. Christians, he says, are no longer completely in the dark about God's plans. In Christ they have at least been shown an outline of what God has in store for all people. So that text actually continues:

What no eye has seen and no ear has heard ... God *has* revealed to us through the Spirit ... For the Spirit we have received is ... God's own Spirit, so that we may understand the lavish gifts God has planned to give us ... (The Old Testament pessimistically asked:) 'Who has ever known the mind of the Lord?' (We optimistically reply that we *can*, because) we have the mind of Christ.

(1 Corinthians 2.9–16)

In other words, Paul is confident that we do not have to remain totally silent about the future. We are still

15

able to say something worthwhile about it. Not on the basis of some private revelation, but on the basis of the experience, common to all Christians, of having received the Spirit of Christ, and so of having entered into the mind of Christ. This experience does not, it is true, provide us with any concrete information about the future; but it does allow us to make a projection on to the future, in the conviction that what we have experienced is eternally and persistently true.

Our language, in that case, will inevitably be couched in the future tense, but it will really be a profound comment on the present. It should not be taken as a description of realities that lie beyond the veil, for that veil remains impenetrable. It is an interpretation of realities that we know have already begun this side of the veil. What talk about 'the end' offers us, however pictorial it may be, is not information about a hidden world, but an interpretation of this world. Like all religious language, it is addressed not to the mind in order to satisfy men's curiosity, but to the heart in order to challenge and change men's understanding of themselves. It is designed to illuminate not just one obscure area of our life, but the whole of it.

THEOLOGICAL UNDERTAKERS

If that is the case, then there is need for a rethinking of the whole of eschatology. Eschatology is that area of theology which deals with the *eschata*, or the 'last things'. In classical theology, the specialist in these matters was regarded as a kind of theological undertaker or mortician. His expertise commanded all the respectful awe (and, let it be said, the suppressed mirth) usually accorded to a funeral director. Those who took his apparent forecasts of the future literally and ventured into even more detailed speculations about the occult were generally regarded as cranks, and often were.

But if the whole of eschatology, however much it seems to talk about the future, is really a comment on the present, then it can no longer be regarded as the preserve of specialists and eccentrics. It concerns all who are trying to understand the world they live in.

It is for this reason that recent theologians, and not merely the funereal ones, have been turning their attention to the 'last things', and asking some searching questions about eschatological language. The purpose of this book is to make their thinking on the subject more accessible than, in the nature of the case, it is. Many Christians have for some time past been asking the same question on their own account, and have felt vaguely guilty about the disloyalty they might be showing. They suspect that, as Christians, they are not allowed to question the traditional teaching in which they were brought up. My aim is to reassure them. They are not being disloyal. On the contrary, they are showing a responsibility which can only be admired. Their questions are no more than the echoes – sometimes even the stimulus – of those which the theologians are asking, and they may be pleasantly surprised to discover how much more radical the scholars have been than they themselves were prepared to be.

THE QUESTION MARK

It goes without saying that the question mark in the title of this book is an essential part of its meaning, as it

17

has been in all the titles of this series.[2] I do not claim to provide answers to the many questions which people ask about the last things, only to stand alongside them in their questioning. I hope to be able to sharpen some of the questions they put, and possibly to add some they had not thought of. I hope to help them distinguish between the right questions and the wrong ones, that is to say, between those that can open us to a new self-understanding and those that can only issue in a dead end.

But I cannot pretend to know the answers to the questions. No one can. However assertively my enthusiasm may make me express myself, I do not want to suggest that the mystery with which we are dealing is anything other than impenetrable. Having scolded those authors who leave one with the impression that the mystery has been solved, it would be strange if I left the reader with the impression that I agreed with them.

[2] See H. J. Richards, *The First Christmas: What Really Happened?*; *The Miracles of Jesus: What Really Happened?*; *The First Easter: What Really Happened?*

2. Death

I mentioned the 'suppressed mirth' often accorded to undertakers. On the stage, and in stories, jokes and songs, the lugubrious mortician has regularly been regarded, throughout man's history, as good for a laugh. Even an amateur psychologist can identify the reason for this: we make fun (among other things) of what we cannot face. What the undertaker stands for – dying, death and decomposition – is too painful for us to contemplate. So we turn to laughter to dissolve our anxiety and, for a time anyway, exorcize the unwelcome ghost.

INTO THE UNKNOWN

'If the rich could hire the poor to die for them, the poor could make a very good living.' The rueful Yiddish proverb accurately points to the universal fear of death, even among those who otherwise enjoy a strong sense of security.

Deep down we all dread death. Not necessarily the actual process of dying which, in the event, if only out of sheer exhaustion, can be a time of comparative calm. What is feared is rather the concept of death, the prospect of life being cut short and coming to an end.

This fear is something quite distinct from the natural resistance to death common to all living beings, which ensures that life goes on against all expectations to the contrary. Even the most inexperienced gardener has discovered the astonishing life force in his battle against weeds. The dread of death lies at a different level, and is more akin to the child's fear of the dark and the unknown. As they grow, some learn to cope with these fears better than others; our sense of security is totally dependent on the environment and upbringing we have enjoyed or been denied. But no one can ever entirely rid himself of the apprehension that is instinctively felt in the face of anything unknown, least of all of something as totally unknown as death. Each man faces his coffin with the sort of feelings motorists know as they reach the traffic signal at the crossroad: 'Do not enter this box unless your exit is clear.' His exit is *not* clear. He can't see that far, and he enters the box with some trepidation.

Some people refuse to admit this fear. This may itself be an indication of how deep-seated their fear really is: it is so threatening that it cannot be allowed to come to the surface. To acknowledge it would be to be overwhelmed by it. So they claim that they are resigned to the inevitability of death, or even that they accept it with equanimity. Some turn the tables completely and speak of their longing for death. The life they have experienced is not worth living, and they are happy to trade it in, even if they get nothing in return. It is revealing that such a death-wish is still regarded in law as evidence of an unsound mind. The treatment accorded to them has made their life more absurd, and therefore more fearful, than death itself.

There are others who, while they honestly admit their fear of death, are ashamed of it. For them, fear is synonymous with cowardice, and they feel it incumbent on them, at least for the sake of others, to hide the panic that grips them at the thought of death. Worst of all, they feel that such dread is un-Christian. To acknowledge it openly would be to deny what they imagine their faith demands of them – a patient acceptance of death, or at least a stiff upper lip. Countless Christian sermons have assured them of this, and Christian hymn-writers have vied with each other to put it to music:

> Away with our sorrow and fear!
> We soon shall recover our home.
> (Charles Wesley)

> But timorous mortals start and shrink
> To cross this narrow sea,
> And linger, shivering on the brink,
> And fear to launch away.
> (Isaac Watts)

> When I tread the verge of Jordan,
> Bid my anxious fears subside.
> (William Williams)

> Why should I shrink at pain and woe,
> Or feel, at death, dismay?
> (Joseph Bromehead)

The language is so much at variance with what the normal person feels in the face of death that one might be forgiven for suspecting that the hymn-writers were never in the presence of a real death, least of all that of Jesus of Nazareth. After all, the New Testament records do not represent him as facing his agony with equanimity; they speak of the sweat coming off him as if he was bleeding. They describe him in one of the New Testament's most moving pages, as:

> feeling our weaknesses with us,
> put to the test in exactly the same way as ourselves . . .

he can sympathize with those who are ignorant
because he too is subject to the limitations of
weakness . . .
During his life on earth
he offered up prayer and entreaty,
with loud cries and with tears
to the one who had the power to save him from death.
(Hebrews 4.15-5.7)

Mark and Matthew even speak of him as breathing his
last with a cry so desperate

My God, my God, why have you forsaken me?
(Mark 15.34)

that Luke, with a rather less robust readership in mind,
felt the need to moderate it to something less shocking.
Would Wesley and Watts have reproached Jesus too as
a timorous mortal, and made encouraging noises to jolly
him along? If Christ faced death with anguish and fear,
why should his followers expect to get by less lightly, or
feel ashamed that the prospect of that great unknown
makes them sweat too?

FINALITY OF DEATH

One of the ways in which people try to cope with their
open or secret fear of death is to pretend it is not really
death at all. What happens at the end is not really an
end but the beginning of something else. The dying
person does not really die, he falls asleep for a while in
order to wake up again later. The disintegration which
he is undergoing will not really do any permanent
damage, it is only temporary. The sorrow and distress

felt by all who witness the scene is really misplaced; they should envy the dead man his good fortune in escaping from this vale of tears to a better life, from this prison to freedom, from this exile to the true homeland.

This theme too has figured strongly in our Christian hymns:

> Brief life is here our portion,
> Brief sorrow, short-lived care:
> The life that knows no ending,
> The tearless life is there.
> O happy retribution:
> Short toil, eternal rest;
> For mortals and for sinners
> A mansion with the blest! . . .
> O home of fadeless splendour,
> Of flowers that bear no thorn,
> Where they shall dwell as children
> Who here as exiles mourn!
>
> (St Bernard of Cluny)

> O how glorious and resplendent,
> Fragile body, shalt thou be,
> When endued with so much beauty,
> Full of health and strong and free,
> Full of vigour, full of pleasure
> That shall last eternally.
>
> (Thomas à Kempis)

> To the weary and the worn
> Tell of realms where sorrows cease;
> To the outcast and forlorn
> Speak of mercy and of peace.
>
> (Bishop Walsham How)

Soon shall come the great awakening,
Soon the rending of the tomb
Then the scattering of all shadows,
And the end of toil and gloom.

(Bernhardt Ingemann)

Shadows gone, break of day,
Real life just begun.
There's no break, there's no end,
Just a living on.

(William Arms Fisher)

We by enemies distrest,
They in Paradise at rest;
We the captives, they the freed.

No longer must the mourners weep,
Nor call departed Christians dead;
For death is hallowed into sleep,
And every grave becomes a bed.

(John Mason Neale)

We must not say
That those are dead who pass away;
From this our world of flesh set free.

Father, in thy gracious keeping
Leave we now thy servant sleeping.

(John Ellerton)

Rejoice for a brother deceased,
Our loss is his infinite gain;
A soul out of prison released,
And freed from its bodily chain.

(Charles Wesley)

The most well-known expression of this theme comes from the great John Donne himself:

> Death, be not proud, though some have called thee
> Mighty and dreadfull, for though art not soe;
> For those whom thou think'st thou dost overthrow,
> Die not, poore death . . .
> One short sleepe past, wee wake eternally,
> And death shall be no more; Death, thou shalt die!
>
> (Holy Sonnets, X)

In other words, we have no need to fear death, because we won't really die or come to an end.

The truth is, of course, that we will. To gloss over this fact is dishonest, and no less so for being thought the Christian thing to do. Human life does come to an end, and however painful the realization of this may be, we do psychological harm to ourselves by taking refuge behind talk of sleep or release or passing on. There is a tragic finality about death which we must take seriously, or it is not death we are talking about. The Christian may wish to add further comments of his own, but unless what he has to say is based on the reality of death, he is building on a lie.

DEATH FUTURE AND DEATH PAST

In the light of such a negative analysis of death, what further useful comment could the Christian possibly have to make?

One of the many comments made by St Paul is worth examining, because it admits quite openly the ambiguity with which he faces the prospect of death. On the one hand, he shares with all men the fear of death, and this disturbs him sufficiently to make him mix his metaphors thoroughly. In the imagery to which he turns, he speaks of the 'heavenly body' which God has prepared for him, the counterpart of the earthly body to which he has become so attached. In his confusion he is not sure whether to compare this body to a tent which one might put up, or a house which one might build, or the clothes which one might wear. What he is sure of is that he does not relish having his earthly body folded up (or demolished as it might be, or stripped off). He would much prefer, if possible, to have his heavenly body superimposed on top of the earthly tent/building/clothes while he is still alive, and so escape the dreaded prospect of dying. He says:

> We are well aware that when the tent that houses us on earth is folded up, there is a house for us from God, not made by human hands but everlasting, in the heavens. And in this earthly state we do indeed groan, longing to put on our heavenly home over the present one; if indeed we are to be found clothed rather than stripped bare. Yes, indeed, in this present tent, we groan under the burden, not that we want to be stripped of our covering, but because we want to be covered with a second garment on top, so that what is mortal in us may be swallowed up by life.
>
> (2 Corinthians 5.1–4)

Even for Paul, the mixture of metaphors is remarkable.

Yet in the very next sentence, he changes his tune entirely. Because in a way our life on earth is an exile from God. It is marked by a sense of God's immeasurable distance, and of our powerlessness to bridge the chasm that separates us from him. If death brings us finally and unequivocally into the presence of God, then there is a sense in which, however unknown that naked

26

confrontation may be, one can only welcome it. The separation which leaves our lives so unfulfilled will be over. So Paul continues:

> We are always full of confidence, realising that as long as we are at home in the body we are exiled from the Lord, guided by faith and not yet by sight; we are full of confidence, then, and long instead to be exiled from the body and to be at home with the Lord. *(ibid.* 5.6–8)

Paul's more optimistic second-thoughts are based on a specifically Christian understanding of the death of Jesus. For his death too seemed to spell his furthest separation from that in which he had grounded his whole life. It was only after profound reflection that his disciples saw it with new eyes, as the moment of his closest union with God. God had not abandoned him, as even he had feared, but had endorsed him as the undistorting mirror of God's own love and forgiveness.

The perfect image of God, Christ was also seen by his followers as the perfect image of man. This was man as he was always meant to be. He was more than an individual: he was representative man, the beginning of a new mankind.

In this interpretation, the death of Jesus was more than the passing away of one good man. It affected all men, because it was something done on behalf of all mankind. Not as if he died in the place of others, to release them from the necessity of dying. On the contrary, his death somehow included the death of all other men. If he died, then they have in a sense died too, and entered into a new order of things. From then on, where they should feel most at home is no longer in the past order, for the death-knell has sounded over that.

Where they really belong now is in the new world that has been opened up, here and now, by the death of Christ. Paul sums up this complex thought a few sentences further on:

> We have reached the conclusion that one man died for all, and therefore all mankind has died. His purpose in dying for all was that men, while still in life, should cease to live for themselves ... With us therefore worldly standards have ceased to count ... When anyone is united to Christ, there is a new world; the old order has gone, and a new order has already begun.
>
> (*Ibid.* 5.14–17) (NEB)

The Christian explicitly commits himself to this new world-view at baptism. For the symbolism of that rite is that he has stepped into Christ's grave to indicate that he counts that death as his own. Paul clarifies this thought elsewhere:

> All of us, when we were baptized into Christ Jesus, were baptized into his death. So by our baptism into his death we were buried with him ... We have been joined to him by dying a death like his ... Our former self was crucified with him ... Having died with Christ ... you must see yourselves as being dead.
>
> (Romans 6.3–11)

If that is the background to Paul's thought in the passage in question, it is no wonder that he regards his death as being, somehow, already in the past. The death he is going to undergo in five (or ten or twenty) years' time he has in fact already died. The grave is not something that lies threateningly in front of him – in a sense it is already behind him. His death is not in the future – it is in the past and in the present, as he tries daily to make that significant baptism of his an ever-present reality:

Always we carry with us in our body the death of Jesus.

(2 Corinthians 4.10)

The prospect of future death will no doubt continue to frighten him. But since that death can be no more than the corroboration of something he has already come to terms with, of something he has had to experience many times throughout life, it no longer poses the threat it once did:

Death, where is your victory? Death, where is your sting?

(1 Corinthians 15.55)

In fact, far from being a loss, the experience of future death can be nothing but gain:

Life to me, or course, is Christ, but then death would be a positive gain.

(Philippians 1.21)

So Paul, having openly admitted his utterly human fear of death, has said that as a Christian he must add a futher comment. In the light of his understanding of Christ's death, he knows that he has already coped with that fear. Death has become for him a gateway to resurrection.

It might seem as if this contradicts what was said

earlier in this chapter. With his talk of resurrection, is not Paul doing exactly the same as the hymn-writers I there took to task, glossing over the stark reality of death, and pretending it isn't really death at all?

He is not. For him death remains death, final and conclusive. If it did not, he could not talk of resurrection. For resurrection, whatever it means, is not a resumption of life after a brief interruption. It is a new creation, *ex nihilo*, out of the nothingness of death. For Paul, death remains an impenetrable darkness. But the darkness is filled with the creative presence of God.

3. The Resurrection of the Body

The previous chapter argued that Christian thinking about death should not simply be expressed in the future tense, but in the past and present too. Does this also go for Christian thinking about resurrection? If what the New Testament says about death is as much to do with the Christian's life now as with his last moments, must the same be said of its talk of resurrection?

FUTURE RESURRECTION

Certainly it is the future tense that Christians must naturally have in mind when they think of resurrection. If the word 'death' means something that is still to come, the word 'resurrection' evolves something still further off. Here and now, like Paul, they groan under the burden of their 'body of flesh', and they look forward to a future when that body will eventually be 'glorified'.

I am suggesting that Christians think like this. Perhaps I should say 'some Christians'. For many are unaware that the Christian hope is indeed for a resurrection of the *body*, as the title of this chapter specifies. The most that many Christians hope for is that their 'soul' will survive death, and they are not at all sure that they really want a bodily resurrection. They have experienced it too often as a barrier to God, and too often seen it become food for worms. They see death, as the hymns I quoted do, as a happy escape from the body, and they cannot conceive of a future hope expressed, however gloriously, in bodily terms.

Christians are not to be blamed for thinking like this. They are simply echoing the theology on which they have been fed, in sermons, in manuals of religious education and in devotional books. It is a theology which splits man into a body and soul, and tells him to mistrust the bodily part because it can hinder the salvation of the more important part, the soul. It teaches him to beware of enjoying life in the world, to be suspicious about bodily pleasure, to feel guilty about the gratification of the senses – for these tie him down to earth, whereas he is made for heaven. It encourages him to despise the body for the sake of the soul. The theology is accurately – if rather flamboyantly – expressed in one of John Donne's funeral elegies:

Thinke further on thy selfe, my Soule, and thinke
How thou at first wast made but in a sinke . . .
Thinke but how poore thou wast, how obnoxious;
Whom a small lumpe of flesh could poyson thus.
This curded milke, this poore unlittered whelpe
My body, could, beyond escape or helpe,
Infect thee with Originall sinne, and thou
Couldst neither then refuse, nor leave it now.
Thinke that no stubborne sullen Anchorit,
Which fixt to a pillar, or a grave, doth sit
Bedded, and bath'd in all his ordures, dwels
So fowly as our Soules in their first-built Cels.
Thinke in how poore a prison thou didst lie
After, enabled but to suck and crie.
Thinke, when 'twas growne to most, 'twas a poore
  Inne,
A Province pack'd up in two yards of skinne . . .

But thinke that Death hath now enfranchis'd thee,
Thou hast thy expansion now, and libertie.
(An Anatomie of the World: The Second Anniversary)

One might be forgiven for imagining that this must be a travesty of the Christian teaching on man. Yet Donne was not saying anything fundamentally different from what has been said by Christian theologians, both before his time and since. The extent to which their contempt for the body was commonly accepted as official Christian teaching may be gathered from the anger it aroused in Nietzsche, who saw the man indoctrinated with these views as:

> a caricature of a human being, like an abortion: he had become a 'sinner', he was in a cage, one had imprisoned him behind nothing but sheer terrifying concepts. There he lay now, sick, miserable, filled with ill-will towards himself; full of hatred for the impulses towards life, full of suspicion of all that was still strong and happy. In short, a 'Christian'.
> *(Twilight of the Idols,* trans. by R. J. Hollingdale, Penguin, 1968, p. 56)

Yet such a theology of man *is* a travesty of the New Testament, as Nietzsche himself suspected. One has only to compare the role of the body as outlined in Donne's poem with the role Paul gives it: the Christian's body is the temple of the Holy Spirit. Obviously, if the human body is a 'sink', a 'dungheap', a 'cell', 'two yards of skin' restricting and infecting the soul, then its resurrection is the last thing anyone would hope for. But for the New Testament (as indeed for the Old) the body is not a barrier to union with God or with man – it is man's lifeline to the rest of creation, and so to God. For man

33

cannot be schizophrenically split into a body *and* a soul. He is an undivided whole, a totality. He is not thought of as *having* a body, but as *being* a body. Hence his union with God, far from demanding the exclusion of the body, cannot be conceived of except in terms of the body. If man's body is not saved, then man is not saved either.

HOPE OF RESURRECTION

This will explain the consistency with which the New Testament expresses a hope not simply for the survival of the disembodied soul, but for the resurrection of the body. According to the gospels, Jesus quite openly aligned himself with the Pharisees in their expectation of a bodily resurrection of the dead (see Mathew 22.30, Luke 14.14; 20.35-36). John expands this expectation into a series of promises:[1]

> In all truth I tell you,
> the hour is coming . . .
> when the dead will hear the voice of the Son of God
> and all who hear it will live. (John 5.25)

> The hour is coming
> when the dead will leave their graves
> at the sound of his voice. (5.28)

> The will of him who sent me
> is that I should lose nothing

---

[1] If indeed all these texts are genuinely John's. Some of them are questioned by some scholars because they seem to be inconsistent with the general drift of the fourth gospel.

of all that he has given to me,
but that I should raise it up on the last day. (6.39)

Anyone who eats my flesh and drinks my blood
has eternal life
and I shall raise that person up on the last day. (6.54)

But it is Paul who is most eloquent on the theme. For
him, bodily death is mankind's ultimate and most fearsome enemy (1 Corinthians 15.26), and the one thing
he looks forward to is when bodily death will be overcome, and:

God raised up the Lord from the dead, and he will
raise us up too by his power.   (*Ibid.* 6.14)

Just as all die in Adam, so in Christ all will be
brought to life.   (*Ibid.* 15.22)

He who raised up the Lord Jesus will raise us up with
Jesus in our turn, and bring us to himself.
                                    (2 Corinthians 4.14)

We believe that Jesus died and rose again, and that in
the same way God will bring with him those who
have fallen asleep in Jesus.   (1 Thessalonians 4.14)

It is this that makes him impatient with anticipation:

The whole creation, until this time, has been groaning in labour pains. And not only that . . . we too are
groaning inside ourselves, waiting with eagerness for
our bodies (and not only our 'souls') to be set free.
                                        (Romans 8.22–23)

While he lives his present life, he is painfully conscious

of the fact that he is sharing daily in the death of Jesus. But that makes him all the more impatient for the future. For he is certain that:

> if we have been joined to him by dying a death like his, so we shall be by a resurrection like his . . . provided that we share his suffering, so as to share his glory. (Romans 6.5; 8.17)

> Moulded to the pattern of his death, striving towards the goal of resurrection from the dead.
> (Philippians 3.10–11)

Ideally, of course, he already belongs to the world where Christ is at one with God. And as a representative of that world to his fellow men, his task is here and now to live the life-style proper to that world. But he is conscious of how poorly he does this, and yearns for the perfection that lies in the future:

> Our homeland is in heaven, and it is from there that we are expecting a Saviour, the Lord Jesus Christ, who will transfigure the wretched body of ours into the mould of his glorious body. (*Ibid.* 3.20–21)

The quotations make it clear how central to Christian thought is the hope of bodily resurrection. Not that 'bodily' is to be understood crudely, as if it had to do with the reanimation of corpses. It shows a gross misunderstanding of the word to speculate (as the medieval theologians did) whether the resurrection body can move from place to place, and whether in doing so it has to pass through the intervening space and through other bodies. The biblical word 'body', as I pointed out earlier, refers to the whole person, not to the relics of him that are buried in the soil. Its English equivalent is not the body which displaces two cubic metres of earth, but the body in words like 'somebody', 'anybody', 'nobody'. It is the whole person, with the network of relationships with all the other bodies that make up the world, that yearns for salvation, completion and perfection. For the failure of man to live up to his calling should not be attributed to the fact that he is 'only human'. His trouble is that he is not human enough. It is not his bodily communication-system with others that frustrates him, but the limitations of that system. He yearns to be fully human, and not in fits and starts. He yearns to be one hundred per cent bodily, not one per cent.[2]

GUARANTEE OF RESURRECTION

But he is able to do even more than yearn, according to the New Testament. For a world in which resurrection bodies exist is not simply a project for the future. It came into being on the first Easter day, and exists here and now as a reality in our midst. And the Christian has been made an inhabitant of that world through his union with the risen Christ. That was the meaning of his baptism.

In other words, the Christian is not to think of Christ's risen body as a reality beyond his reach, or outside his experience. For Christ is the 'first-born from the dead' (Colossians 1.18), and he cannot be called that unless he is the elder brother of a whole family (Romans 8.29). He is the 'first-fruits' of the dead (1 Corinthians

[2] I have tried to give a fuller analysis of the biblical word 'body', and of the implication for Christ's resurrection and our own, in ch. 6 of *The First Easter: What Really Happened?*

15.20), and this implies that there is a whole harvest ready and waiting to be reaped.

Christ therefore, in his risen body, *is* the resurrection of Christians (John 11.25), infusing into their bodies a life against which death cannot hold out. The New Testament speaks of him as pouring his immortal and incorruptible Spirit into men's bodies. That Spirit must be seen as a 'seed' which will, in the nature of things, produce an incorruptible fruit (Romans 8.23), or, better still, as the 'pledge' – the first instalment or down-payment which is the guarantee of what is to follow (2 Corinthians 1.22; 5.5, Ephesians 1.14).

For Christians, therefore, their own resurrection is not simply a desirable possibility, or a future proba-bility. It is guaranteed. And not as something 'miraculous' which will uncannily happen to them, some weird and unannounced change they will undergo. It will simply be the inevitable flowering of their baptism, when the resurrection of Christ within them fully asserts itself. Christ's victory over death will become their own, because they are part of Christ. Anything other than that would be unthinkable. Paul writes:

You are not 'in the flesh', but 'in the Spirit', since the Spirit of God has made a home in you . . . And if the Spirit of him who raised Jesus from the dead has made his home in you, then he who raised Jesus from the dead (cannot do otherwise than) give life to your own mortal bodies, through his Spirit (already) living in you.   (Romans 8.9–11)

Christians therefore refuse to express their hope in merely individualistic terms. Because they are essen-tially bodily, they are tied – body and soul, as we say –

38

to the rest of creation. Their salvation, however it is to be envisaged, cannot be thought of apart from the salvation of the whole. They cannot be redeemed out of the mass, but only in and with it. Their salvation cannot be other than corporate and communal, and will be essentially incomplete until all their brothers and sisters are included. How can anyone regard himself as finally happy until all are? The point is gently put by St Symeon of Russia:

> I know a man who desired the salvation of his brethren so fervently that he often besought God with burning tears and with his whole heart that either his brethren might be saved with him, or he might be condemned with them. For he was bound to them in the Holy Spirit by such a bond of love that he did not even wish to enter the kingdom of heaven if to do so meant to be separated from them.

RESURRECTION NOW

Yet even that does not fully express the Christian hope of resurrection. For, in the last analysis, the good news is not that the resurrection of the body is a guaranteed future bonus, but that it is a present reality. The risen body of Christ into which their baptism has incorporated them, and on which they 'feed' in communion, is not merely something they wait for, but hold in their hands. The body of Christ, victorious over death, exists not merely in the past and in the future, but here and now. For it is nothing other than the church.

The Christian is not to think of the church as separate from Christ, directed and guided by him from a distance. It is his body, his manner of continuing to exist among men. And the Christian is one of the many members or limbs of that body. Paul spoke of a heavenly body which he hoped to 'put on' at his resurrection. On second thoughts, he had to admit that this he had already done, for that body was nothing other than the church of which he already formed part. The resurrection body which is so central to the Christian's hope is not something different from the community of Christians which we call the 'body of Christ': they are the same thing, and they are a reality in the present, not the future.

To the future tenses quoted above, therefore, Paul is able to add the following past and present tenses:

> The ones God destined to be moulded to the pattern of his Son . . . he has (already) brought into glory.
>
> (Romans 8.29-30)

> God has appointed Christ as supreme head to the church, which is his body and as such holds within it (here and now) the fullness of him who himself receives the entire fullness of God.
>
> (Ephesians 1.22-23, NEB)

> God, through the great love with which he loved us . . . brought us to life with Christ . . . and (has already) raised us up with him and given us a place with him in heaven. (*Ibid.* 2.6)

> By your baptism, you have (already) been raised up with Christ . . . You were dead . . . he has brought you to life with him. (Colossians 2.12–13)

Since you have (already) been raised up to be with Christ, you must look for the things that are above, where Christ is. (*Ibid.* 3.1)

The New Testament sees the church as a part of creation that has already been released from the corruption which it is by nature subject. The world is not a quarry out of which some entirely different building is being constructed elsewhere. It is an extension of people's bodies, and when people are being redeemed the redemption of the whole world has here and now begun. So the church is the beginning of a new creation, and Christians, with their death and resurrection already behind them, must see themselves as part of that world renewed. The 'eternal life' proper to risen bodies is not something they hope to enjoy in another existence. It is a present reality, as the fourth gospel repeatedly emphasizes:

Whoever believes in the one who sent me,
has eternal life . . .
and has (already) passed from death to life.
(John 5.24)

In all truth I tell you,
the hour is coming – indeed it is here already –
when the dead will hear the voice of the Son of God,
and all who hear it will live. (5.25)

Eternal life is this (present reality):
to know you,
the only true God,
and Jesus Christ whom you have sent. (17.3)

We have (already) passed over from death to life . . .
because we love our brothers. (1 John 3.14)

4. Heaven and Eternal Life

At an early stage of my Christian education, I remember being told to imagine eternity in terms of a bird which comes once every million years to scratch its beak on the summit of Mt Everest. When this remarkable bird had eventually worn the mountain down to nothing, the first minute of eternity would have elapsed.

I have to admit that the thought of eternity as time going on and on, without respite for ever and ever, did not make a very strong appeal to my youthful imagination. I no longer have nightmares at the prospect, but it still tends to make my head swim and induce a feeling of nausea. Nor have the intervening years endeared the image to me any the more. In fact, the only time I came across an image I found less appealing was in a sermon, where the preacher asked us to think of all the happiness we had ever known as if it were a single grain of sand. Heaven, he promised us, would be like a whole desert . . .

WORLD WITHOUT END

'If hevens such a nice place', writes a six-year-old in a recent collection of children's writing, 'why are poeple so sad about going there?' Perhaps because the prospect of such endless boredom would make even an angel wilt.

It is unfortunate, though perhaps inevitable, that the words we use to express the kind of life that people might live 'after' death are all taken from our experience of time. We speak of 'everlasting' life, and imagine a life that lasts on for an infinite period of time. We speak of life that is 'perpetual' or 'permanent', and conjure up an image of life that perdures, remains, continues beyond where other things stop. The very word eternal, etymologically, means nothing more than 'going on for ages'.[1]

True enough, we turn very naturally to negative words to convey the fact that we really don't know what it is we are describing, only what it is not. So God's life is spoken of as unlimited, unbounded, immortal, infinite, imperishable, unending; and what we mean is that it is not like *our* life – limited, bounded, mortal, finite, doomed to perish and come to an end. But even in these negative instances we are still thinking of God's 'time' as going on beyond the confines of our time. Our world comes to an end; God lives in a world without end.

In actual fact, of course, God does not fit into the category of time at all. It isn't as if he has much more of it than we have, an 'infinite' amount. It is that time simply doesn't come into the question. God, to be God, is outside of time. He does not, like us, have a past and a future. He transcends time. He is timeless.

When we speak of God's eternal or everlasting life, therefore, we should not be thinking of how (infinitely) long it lasts. The word may be clumsy, but it is trying to say something about the quality of God's life, not the quantity. God lives a life which, by definition, is free of all the restrictions with which we know our own lives beset. Not only the restrictions of time, but all the other limitations we experience, of incompleteness, mediocrity, impoverishment, superficiality, shabbiness, con-

[1] *Aeternus* comes from the latin *aetas,* and *aionios* from the Greek *aion.* Both mean an age.

straint, instability. God's life is complete, full, rich, deep, glorious, free, unwavering.

Such is the life we all yearn for. And we could not yearn for it if we had not, in our best moments, already tasted something of it. There is no one who has not experienced, even if only minimally, how full and rich life can be. In such experiences, even time becomes an irrelevant factor. It is not that we had much more than our usual share of it. On the contrary, the experience may, in terms of time, have lasted only for a short while. But while it lasted, we were no longer conscious of time. We realized that time is only one of the dimensions we live in, and that we can live in dimensions which can't be measured in hours or years, even if they were multiplied to infinity. We experienced the timelessness of eternity because we managed, if only for a while, to live as God does, totally in the present tense.

WORLD TO COME

The New Testament promises that this timeless dimension, which man has already experienced and which he yearns for, can become his in a definitive way. Under a variety of titles – heaven, glory, eternal life, kingdom, paradise – it promises a future in which men are so close to God that they will live his kind of life. Indeed, in many instances, it distinguishes the present 'age' from the 'age to come' when this will be so. This means that the phrase 'eternal life' often refers not to a life which goes on 'for ages', but to the life of 'the age (to come)'. Eternal life is the new world that awaits man in the future.

There can be no denying that a heaven which still lies in the future features strongly in the New Testament. The gospels speak of the 'kingdom where the upright will shine like the sun' (Matthew 13.43), and of the 'other age' when those who have been raised from the dead will no longer die (Luke 20.34). They speak of a future treasure (Matthew 19.21) and of a reward in heaven (5.12), and promise a judgement in which the upright will be granted 'eternal life' (25.46) in the 'age to come' (Mark 10.30).

St Paul too, at least in some texts, finds little difficulty in distinguishing between his present experiences of earth and his hope of heaven, and every aching bone of his body assures him that he is still on earth and not yet in heaven:

We hold this treasure (the gospel) in pots of earthenware . . . We are subjected to every kind of hardship . . . We see no way out . . . pursued . . . knocked down . . . Always we carry with us in our body the death of Jesus . . . We are continually being handed over to death . . . In us, death is at work . . .

But we do not waver; indeed, though this outer human nature of ours may be falling into decay, at the same time our inner human nature is renewed day by day. The temporary, light burden of our hardships is earning for us (in the future) an utterly incomparable, eternal weight of glory.

(2 Corinthians 4.7–17)

He is prepared to put up with the present sorrows for the sake of that glorious future:

In my estimation, all that we suffer in the present time is nothing in comparison with the glory which is destined to be disclosed for us.   (Romans 8.18)

But until that 'age to come' has arrived, he knows that he is far from heaven, and thinks of himself, as we have seen as 'exiled from the Lord' (2 Corinthians 5.6).

HEAVEN ON EARTH

Yet in other texts he says almost the opposite. For in one sense that 'age to come' has already arrived. It arrived on Easter day, with the risen Christ. For to live a life beyond death, a life that is free and no longer threatened by death – this is to live the life of the 'age to come'. And when people became aware that such a life was being lived in their midst by one who just a short while before was mortal like themselves, they knew that the 'age to come' was no longer in the future, but had arrived.

Paul sees that risen Christ as the beginning of a new creation. He is a second Adam (1 Corinthians 15.45), the 'New Man' (Ephesians 2.15) finally fulfilling God's specifications, 'created in God's likeness, in true goodness and holiness' (Ephesians 4.24). As such, he is not simply an individual wonderman; he is the prototype of a new mankind. The whole human race is destined to follow that pattern. And in Paul's thinking, this process has already begun. For it is one of his favourite themes that Christians are not just followers of Christ, looking up to him as their leader and exemplar; they are *in* Christ.[2] They are therefore already swept up into the

[2] Paul almost murders language to emphasize this. It is commonly thought that 'the Greeks had a word for it', but they did not have one for what Paul wanted to say, and he coined eighty-six new words to express the fact that the Christian 'withsuffers' with Christ, is 'with-crucified' with him, 'withdies' with him, is 'withburied, withraised, and made withalive' with him, 'withreigns and is withglorified' with him, etc.

new creation that was inaugurated on Easter day. Christians, being in Christ, cannot here and now be other than where Christ is: in heaven even while they are still on earth, in glory even while they feel little like it, in the age to come even while they know with every bone in their body that they are still in the present age:

For anyone who is in Christ, there is a new creation; the old order is gone, and the new one is here.
(2 Corinthians 5.17)

The Father of our Lord Jesus Christ has blessed us with all the spiritual blessings of heaven in Christ.
(Ephesians 1.3)

Those whom God destined to be moulded to the pattern of his Son . . . he has brought into glory.
(Romans 8.29-30)

Our Lord Jesus Christ gave himself for our sins to liberate us from this present wicked age (and place us in the future age). (Galatians 1.4)

If you have really died with Christ to the principles of this world, why do you act as though you were still living in the world? (Colossians 2.20)

In short the new creation, or world to come, is not simply a future reality for which people may yearn. In the church, which is the body of the risen Christ, people have already entered it. The power of the 'age to come' has already been released in the bodies of those who together form the body of Christ.

This means that heaven ought not to be thought of as the antithesis of earth, so alien to earth and 'out of this world' that one has to be destroyed for the other to take its place. On the contrary, says Paul:

> The whole creation has been groaning (not in expectation of being destroyed but) in labour pains ... God's intention is that the whole creation itself might be freed from its slavery to corruption and brought into the same glorious freedom as the children of God.
>
> (Romans 8.22, 21)

Earth gives way to heaven, not by disappearing but by being transformed. And this transformation of our world was guaranteed when the Jesus of the flesh was transformed into the Christ of glory by the power of God. For this was not some isolated 'miracle'. The risen Christ was revealed as the focal point of the whole of creation, the model on which every other act of creation had been based. The plan is, and always was, that all creatures should become as he is. And that plan is already in operation, in the church.

The church, therefore, as the previous chapter already suggested, is not to be thought of as the gathering of an elect *out of* a world which is going to be written off. The church *is* the world already in process of being transformed in accordance with God's plan. At least, that is how the New Testament hopefully envisages it. Just as Paul speaks of the risen Christ as the 'firstfruits' of a whole harvest of transformed Christians (1 Corinthians 15.20), so James describes Christians as the 'firstfruits' of an entire transformed creation (James 1.18). The church stands among men as the witness of a transformation in which all are to share.

Christians least of all ought to talk of the heaven that men hope for as some unknown quantity. For Christians it cannot be something new, in the sense of different from what they already know. It can only be the clear and explicit manifestation of something they have already experienced, though in the darkness of faith:

> The life you have is hidden with Christ in God. But when Christ is revealed – and he is your life – you too will be revealed with him in glory.
>
> (Colossians 3.3-4)

LIFE BEFORE DEATH

This New Testament emphasis on the present needs to be reinstated in those areas where Christianity is thought to be mainly concerned with a post-mortem life of the future. It is widely imagined, not least by Christians themselves, that Jesus directed men's gaze to a God who was elsewhere not here, to a life that was to be lived later not now, and to a hope that was to be fulfilled in another world not this one. It is a type of Christianity that is well summed up in the dictum: 'Serve the Lord; the pay isn't much, but the retirement benefits are out of this world.'

Such a Christianity has little to do with the preaching of Jesus as the New Testament has reported it. For what he proclaimed was not the 'heaven' of popular imagination, but the Kingdom of 'The Heavens', that is to say, of God.[3] And this Kingdom, he said, was not only imminent but already in operation through his preaching. Indeed, in parable after parable he made it clear that for him the phrase represented a vision of life as it

[3]It is not widely enough known that 'The Heavens' is a reverential paraphrase for God, common in late Old Testament Judaism, and that Matthew's regular phrase 'Kingdom of The Heavens' should really be translated 'Kingdom of God'.

should be lived, urgently demanding here and now a decision from his audience, because the only time for bringing about such a life was now.

So aware was St John of this existential character of the gospel that he replaced the word 'Kingdom' in Jesus's preaching with the words 'eternal life' meaning, as we have seen, not a life which goes on for a long time, but a life which is characteristic of God. This life is for the taking here and now, and the following texts should be added to those at the end of the preceding chapter to drive the point home:

God gave his only Son
so that everyone who believes in him . . .
may *have* eternal life. (John 3.16)

Anyone who believes in the Son
has eternal life. (3.36)

The bread of God
is the bread which comes down from heaven
and gives life to the world . . .
I *am* the bread of life. (6.33-35)

Everyone who believes
has eternal life. (6.47)

Anyone who eats my flesh and drinks my blood
has eternal life. (6.54)

I have come
so that they may *have* life
and have it to the full. (10.10)

The sheep that belong to me listen to my voice . . .
I *give* them eternal life.   (10.28)

I *am* . . . the Life.   (14.6)

Believing this (that Jesus is the Son of God)
you *have* life through his name.   (20.31)

God has *given* us eternal life
and this life is in his Son;
whoever has the Son *has* life.   (1 John 5.11–12)

It may be objected that this talk of a God-like life
that may be enjoyed here and now is almost as unreal-
istic as the 'pie in the sky' which it is hopefully meant to
replace. 'Heaven on earth' may make sense to the few
who find fulfilment in their relationships and their
work, but it must sound like a bad joke to the many
whose lives are empty and cramped, who know little or
nothing of freedom or fulfilment, and who are unlovely
simply because they live and die unloved. How can we
speak of heaven in the present tense to the diseased and
the bedridden, to the undernourished and the
oppressed, to the maladjusted and the handicapped, to
the broken and the inadequate – or even to the ordin-
arily lonely and depressed?

The question may be answered with another question: what sort of solution is it to the suffering of these
people to promise them a fulfilled life later? How honest
is it to assure people that they will eventually be healed
by love – even by the love of God – if they have never
experienced that healing love from us here and now?

Obviously large numbers of people experienced little
in the way of 'eternal life' in their day-to-day existence.
But to conclude that therefore they will be compensated

in another world is a form of despair. The real believer is the one who accepts responsibility for that situation, and declares himself ready to change it. For to believe in eternal life is to believe in a life on earth which really *is* life, not half death, and to declare that it can renew our history because it has palpably done so again and again. To believe in eternal life is to face all the evil and misery of our history, and to proclaim that the powers of renewal are stronger. To believe in eternal life is to accept the task our world imposes on us, which is to summon it out of its many moments of death to the new life guaranteed to it by the God who raised Jesus from death.

HEAVENS ABOVE

This vision of a fullness of life which is hoped for and fought for *within* history and in *our* world stands in stark contrast with the Christian hymns quoted above, which have largely despaired of history and projected their hopes for fulfilment into a speculative *other* world *beyond* history. A heaven here below is not on. The only safe bet is a heaven above.

It is not as if these hymns did not have biblical warrant: they have done little more than enlarge on the imagery already authoritatively established in the famous vision with which the New Testament closes, in the Book of Revelation. There, heaven is presented as so otherworldly and beyond human conceiving that it requires an opening of doors hitherto sealed in order to reveal its mysteries to the privileged viewer.

In the centre of this heaven stands the throne of God, set on a sea of crystal and illuminated by rainbows and lightning. The throne is guarded by four sphinx-like creatures, and encircled by a court of twenty-four crowned elders, myriads of singing angels, and a host of worshipping believers beyond counting (Revelation 4-7). In a further vision, the whole complex is called the New Jerusalem, and described as a cube (or pyramid?) of solid gold covering two million square miles, transparent as glass and radiant as a jewel. It is surrounded by diamond walls set on foundations faced with precious stones. It is entered by twelve angelic gates, illuminated by the radiance of God, and watered by a miraculously lifegiving stream issuing from the throne in the city centre (chapter 21).

If a heaven of such splendour is obviously not of this world, not even in the ideal future, why blame the hymn-writers for presuming that it must exist in another world? Because they too clumsily take as literal description what is plainly meant to be symbolic. The New Jerusalem is no more a factual description of what will be than solid gold can factually be transparent, or a city factually extend from London to Rome, or from Washington to New Orleans.

The author of the Book of Revelation has not got a giant telescope trained on some other world, even though sometimes he writes as if he had. This is a licence we must allow him as a poet. His imagery is in fact taken entirely from this world – where else could he take it from? Through the categories of size, numbers, symmetry, gems, jewellery and precious metals, he tries to evoke the idea of perfection. This perfection he and his readers have already experienced – how else could they understand each other? – though only fitfully and elusively.

To build up that present experience into an absolute is not to despair of the present. On the contrary, it is to reaffirm most powerfully the harmony which can and will reign here on earth for life to be worthy of God. Indeed, paradoxically, the New Jerusalem of the vision is not in another world; it 'comes down from God out of heaven' (21.2) to transform the earth, not to displace it. For God is one who says, 'I am making the whole of creation new' (21.5), and the man of faith sees that promise already at work.

The basic biblical image of heaven and eternal life therefore, even in the florid imagery of the Book of Revelation, is not of an escape into another world, but of the transformation of our world in such a way that we are no longer distant from God. For the believer, this is what heaven eventually will be, and in fact already is. For some, of course, such a prospect could seem like hell, and this is the topic we must now turn to.

5. Judgement and Hell

In a Mel Calman cartoon, God is as always sitting on a cloud. This time he is looking rather threateningly on his faithful below, and admonishing them: 'Love each other, or I'll come and do you!'

Most God cartoons have a serious point to make, and this is no exception. We smile at the concept of a God who can only make men as loving as he is by waving his fist at them. But there is good biblical warrant for the anomaly. A beautiful Old Testament text is anxious to instil in Israel God's own loving concern for the poor:

> You will not molest or oppress aliens, for you your-
> selves were once aliens in Egypt. You will not illtreat
> widows or orphans ... If they appeal to me, I shall
> listen. At least with me they will find compassion!
>
> (Exodus 22.21ff.)

But it finishes as paradoxically as the cartoon:

> I shall certainly hear their appeal; my anger will be
> roused and I shall put you to the sword.   (22.24)

Nor is this phenomenon confined to the Old Testament. Christians readily quote the tender words of the fourth gospel:

> This is how God loved the world:
> he gave his only Son,
> so that everyone who believes in him may not perish
> but may have eternal life.   (John 3.16)

But few follow the quotation through to its conclusion:

Whoever does not believe is judged. (3.18)

Clearly these texts regard judgement and condemnation as an essential counterpart of salvation: talk of heaven is incomplete until a word has also been said about hell. God's love is misunderstood if it is not balanced by God's justice.

JUDGEMENT DAY

It would seem, then, as if the theme of judgement is not in opposition to the theme of love. On the contrary, it is suggested, without judgement love would be trivialized. A God defined only in terms of love would have no muscle. The definition would fail to spell out the burning passion that love is, and the demands it makes on both lover and beloved. Can a God who only loves, and never passes judgement, be taken seriously? Does he not inevitably become a benign uncle who smiles indulgently on the children as long as they are happy? All sense of the awesomeness of God – of his holiness, as the Bible calls it – would be lost. So would all sense of the enormity of evil, as if it did not really matter, and could easily be forgiven.

The hymn-writers, if we may turn to them again, have not failed to orchestrate this theme too, perhaps to make up for their over-enthusiasm for death. If judgement lies beyond death, one should perhaps approach it rather more cautiously than some of the earlier hymns recommended!

His chariots of wrath the deep thunderclouds form,
And dark is his path on the wings of the storm.

(Robert Grant)

Thou Judge of quick and dead,
Before whose bar severe,
With holy joy, or guilty dread,
We all shall soon appear;
Our cautioned souls prepare
For that tremendous day . . .
To pray, and wait the hour,
That awful hour unknown.   (Charles Wesley)

That day of wrath, that dreadful day
When heaven and earth shall pass away;
What power shall be the sinner's stay?
How shall we meet that dreadful day? . . .
O! On that day, that wrathful day,
When man to judgement wakes from clay.
                        (Thomas of Celano's *Dies Irae*,
                                trans. by Walter Scott)

It is not as if these dark forebodings sprang from the
morbid imagination of the hymn-writers. They have
good biblical precedent. The Old Testament prophets in
particular look forward in awed anticipation to that
'Day of the Lord', beyond history, when men will no
longer be able to avoid confrontation with God, and
must render an account of their actions. The psalms too
are full of appeals to God as Judge, imploring him to
hasten that Day on behalf of the exploited and
oppressed.

Some pages of the New Testament echo this Old
Testament theme closely. Matthew fills the Baptist's
preaching with dire warnings about the 'wrath to come'
(Matthew 3.7ff.), and the words of Jesus to those who
reject his teaching are couched in the same threatening
terms:

It will be more bearable for Sodom on Judgement
Day than for you.   (Matthew 11.24)

When you have (made a convert) you make him twice
as fit for hell as you are.   (23.15)

Brood of vipers, how can you escape being condemned to hell?   (23.33)

Indeed, the warnings of future punishment are not
addressed to disbelievers only: the possibility of condemnation hangs over everyone, as is made clear in a
number of parables. For all will have to render an
account for the talents they have misused (Matthew
25.14-30), and at the end of the world all who have
done evil will be thrown like darnel 'into the blazing
furnace, where there will be weeping and grinding of
teeth' (Matthew 13.38-42). This judgement will take
place at the end of history, when those 'on the left
hand' will be condemned for their insensitivity and
hardheartedness, and consigned to 'eternal punishment' (Matthew 25.31-46).
There are pages, too, in the epistles which put the
same emphasis on future judgement. Paul writes to
Rome about 'that Day of retribution when God's just
verdicts will be made known' (Romans 2.5), and the
writer of the epistle to the Hebrews warns his readers
against apostasy by holding before them the 'dreadful
prospect of judgement' when the fiery wrath of the
Lord' will exact a severe penalty from the defectors who
'fall into the hands of the living God' (Hebrews
10.26.31). The theme of a dreaded future Judgement
Day is never far below the surface in the New Testament writings.

Yet there are pages which present the theme in a totally
different light. For the gist of the Good News preached
by Jesus was that, in one sense at least, the long antici-
pated Day of the Lord had arrived. The 'last things',
which all men instinctively postpone to a time beyond
history, had strangely come to pass in the midst of
history. The judgement which the whole Old Testament
awaited with bated breath had been passed in the life
and death of Jesus. The New Testament had turned all
the future tenses of the prophets into the present, and
once the Christ-event had taken place, there was really
nothing more that could be added. The fearful 'Retribution which is coming' was not to materialize after all;
Jesus had delivered people from it (1 Thessalonians
1.10).

This emphasis on a 'realized eschatology', as I mentioned earlier, is strongest in the fourth gospel. There,
often in deliberate contrast with the other three gospels,
all the 'last things' are brought uncompromisingly into
the present. Not only is death a reality of everyday life,
and resurrection, and eternal life; judgement is too.

For the purpose of Jesus's presence in the world was
not the negative one of condemnation, either now or in
the future:

God sent his Son into the world
not to judge the world,
but so that through him the world might be saved.

(3.17)

I judge no one. (8.15)

If anyone hears my words
and does not keep them faithfully,

it is not I who shall judge such a person,
since I have not come to judge the world,
but to save the world.   (12.47)

And of course, if Jesus does not judge, neither does
God, for Jesus does not come to show us how different
he is from God, but how alike. Where then does judgement come in, and what does it consist of?

The judgement is this:
though the light has come into the world
people have preferred
darkness to the light . . .
(so that) whoever does not believe
is judged already.   (3.19, 18)

In other words, condemnation is not something
inflicted by God, in response to men's unbelief. That
unbelief is itself their condemnation. They pronounce
judgement on themselves by their response to God's
gift. And if Jesus is the supreme gift of God, then men
are judged – that is, they declare themselves – by their
acceptance or refusal of him.

That is why the death of Jesus, which represents the
outright and final rejection of him by the 'Prince of this
world', is described as the world's Judgement Day.
There it has been shown up for what it truly is, and
stands self-condemned:

Now is the Judgement of the world;
now the Prince of this world is to be driven out.

                                                        (12.31)

All the evangelists describe Jesus's death in terms borrowed from the Old Testament passages about the future Day of the Lord.

Judgement Day is therefore not simply something that will take place in the future. In the deepest sense it is a reality which has already taken place, and which continues to take place daily as men confront the love of God embodied in Jesus Christ. To refuse that love (whether it bears the name of Christ or not) is to opt for self-destruction. It is only in this sense that Jesus can be represented as saying:

> It is for judgement
> that I have come into this world.   (John 9.39)

But it is a judgement that people pass on themselves, every day of their lives. Jesus does not himself condemn, or threaten God's condemnation. On the contrary, he is the sacrament of God's pardon.

FREE PARDON

What does it mean to say that Jesus's life and preaching manifest a God who grants men a free pardon? Perhaps the implications can be most clearly opened out by considering the various responses God could make to sin.

1. At one extreme, he could react by exploding with anger. To have one of his divine orders disregarded is a blatant insult. He blazes with indignation and is determined to take his revenge. In his rage, he smites the sinner with a thunderbolt and so takes his retribution. That will teach him!

2. Alternatively, God's response could be less extreme. He will not give vent to his wrath. He will control his rage. He will be calm and cool – but also

just. What has happened has disturbed good order, and it is essential that the balance be restored. But it will be done with strict equity. Satisfaction must be made, in the precise sense of *satis*: 'enough' to compensate for the injuries perpetrated. Retaliation must take place, in the strict sense of *talis*: 'as much' repayment as the damage done.

3. Or his reaction could be even less severe. He will show generosity and demand far less than is in justice due to him. In fact he will go so far as to demand nothing in repayment for the injury done to him: he will pardon the sinner – but on condition. He must repent, promise never to do it again, and show that his change of heart is sincere. God's pardon is genuine, but it comes in the form of a contract. He forgives on condition that there is repentance and faith on the part of the sinner. That is his side of the bargain. Without that, there is no pardon.

4. Finally we reach the other extreme. God could be so undemanding that he forgives totally and freely, with no conditions attached. His attitude to the sinner will be no different now to what it was before the sin was committed. The relationship remains one of unchanging love, and he acts towards the sinner exactly as if he had not sinned. He turns a blind eye to the sinner's transgression and refuses to pay him back in his own coin, even if he is bent on doing it all over again. God remains utter forgiveness, free and unconditional.

Most people find the first reaction – that of revenge – so repulsive that they reject it, not only as a basis for their own conduct, but for God's too. Their experience of God bears witness to the fact that he is not vindictive, however much they feel at times they would like him to be. And, on balance, the Bible supports their conclusion.

Most people find the last of the four reactions – that of free pardon – so incredible that they reject that too. To have a God as totally forgiving as that is not far removed from having no God at all. And the mere thought of that is so frightening that they put it out of their minds. An unconditional forgiveness is both too good to be true, and too fearful to contemplate.

Most people, therefore, presume that God reacts to sin in one of the two ways between these extremes. If they are by nature aggressive or severe, they will opt for the God of strict justice. If they are constitutionally gentle and mild, they will put their money on the God who forgives, if only conditionally.

Such people may be surprised to discover that the New Testament totally repudiates these two images of God. For if God forgives people *because* they have made satisfaction, or *because* they have repented and believed, then they have earned their forgiveness. And such a concept of 'works' is totally alien to the gospel's liberating message of God's 'grace'. God's forgiveness is given *gratis*, free and unearned. He makes his sun shine on his friends and on his enemies. It is sinners whom he acquits and sends away free, not those who have already worked their way back into his favour. They are not forgiven because *they* are good, but because *he* is good. He loves the world before it repents, not because it deserves his love, just as Jesus refused to condemn the adulterous woman, whether she later repented or not.

Twelve-year-olds are perhaps more capable of understanding this than most adults seem to be. A friend of mine told her class at school the parable of the Prodigal Son up to a point where the father receives the errant youth back home. To his words of welcome she added the proviso, 'on condition that you promise never to do it again'. The children, already familiar with the story, protested that it did not say that. She agreed, but asked if it were not implied in the father's forgiveness. The children, to a man, insisted that if this were so, the whole story was pointless. They had got the message.

Another friend reminds me that, in fact, theological insight takes place at an even earlier stage. He wrote to tell me of the theological questions which his three-year-old daughter is beginning to ask. 'Will you *always* love me', she enquired anxiously after a naughty spell, 'even if I don't love you?' If the father's answer must be yes, how could anyone doubt that the Father of our Lord Jesus Christ loves unwaveringly and unconditionally, even when his will is thwarted or his love spurned?

Nor should we imagine that this is an exclusively New Testament understanding of God. People brought up exclusively on the Old Testament can have just as merciful an idea of God, as witness the following commandments for God (not *of* God) taken from an anonymous tenth century Hebrew acrostic:

> Thou shalt not despise the poor wretch who implores thee for mercy.
> Thou shalt not grieve him or shame him over his sin.
> Thou shalt not remember against him his past sins, hidden in his heart.
> Thou shalt not banish him who strays, but shalt draw near him. *(Penguin Book of Hebrew Verse,* ed. T. Carmi, 1981, p. 247)

GOD'S JUSTICE

What happens, then, to the idea of God's justice? If God does not condemn sinners, but pardons them whether they repent or not, how can he be called a just God?

What greater injustice could there be than to acquit the guilty, to make no distinction between them and the innocent, and to treat them both alike? Are we to assume that God is *not* just, in the way that we understand the word?

Perhaps. Certainly the justice of God spoken of in the Bible has little in common with the world of ideas associated with human justice, namely fair play, setting the balance right, redress, giving to each his deserts, the impartial and dispassionate exactment of the pound of flesh that is due. In fact the biblical word usually means the very opposite of all this. Justice is not the antithesis of mercy: the words are synonymous. This is clear from the frequency with which the words 'justice' or 'righteousness' are put, Hebrew fashion, in parallel with the words 'mercy' or 'love':

The Lord loves uprightness and justice,
the faithful love of the Lord fills the earth.

(Psalm 33.5)

Justice and Judgement the foundations of your throne,
Love and Constancy march before you.

(Psalm 89.14)

I will sing of faithful love and judgement.

(Psalm 101.1)

In your faithful love, O Lord, listen to my voice,
Let your judgements give me life . . .

(Psalm 119.149)

They will bring out the memory of your great generosity,
and joyfully acclaim your justice . . .

Just in all that he does,
the Lord acts only in faithful love.

(Psalm 145.7, 17)

I shall betroth you in uprightness and justice,
and faithful love and tenderness.　　　(Hosea 2.21)

In short, according to the Bible, God's justice is totally
misunderstood if it is thought to be analogous to human
justice. God is just, not when he acts in accordance with
some external norm, but when he acts in accordance
with his own nature. And his nature is to forgive, to
have pity, to save, to come to the rescue of the needy,
whether they are deprived or depraved. His justice is
not judgemental. He is not loving *and also* (occasionally
and regretfully) just. He is always loving *because* he is
always just, that is to say, just to himself as the lover of
mankind. The Byzantine liturgy expresses this perfectly
in one of its Octo-Echos hymns:

Because of our many sins,
where shall we hide, O Lord?
In the heavens?
There resides your majesty and your glory!
In the bottom of the earth?
There your hand is all powerful!
Even in the caves of the earth
your presence is all-pervading.
We rather come to you, O merciful Lord,
and hide in the palm of your hand,
for your love is immeasurable
and your tenderness without limit.

The Russian film *Rublev* expressed the same theme
in a moving sequence where the artist is commissioned

o cover a wall of a new church with an immense Last Judgement. He is told to include plenty of devils to put the fear of God into the congregation. The film shows him agonizing for months, unable to begin to portray such a scene. When he is asked why, he replies, 'What has such a scene to do with the gospel?'

THE WRATH OF GOD

That having been said, it remains true that there are many texts, in the Old and New Testament alike, which are not open to the misunderstanding I have just mentioned. They speak not only of God's justice, but quite uncompromisingly of his wrath, anger, vengeance and threatened retribution. No problem about him being judgemental in these texts!

It would be easy to fill this chapter with texts of this kind. They are legion. Nor have Christians been slow to capitalize on them. The legendary Scottish preacher pictures sinners as crying out in desperation, 'Lord, we didna ken'. 'Well,' replies the Almighty as he consigns them to hell, 'ye ken the noo.'

I have before me a sheaf of stencilled handouts, sent by some kind benefactor, the transcript, I am assured, or revelations recently received from heaven. In undeviating block capitals, and with a fine disregard for spelling and grammar (but then we are dealing with a translation), they consign various categories of people to the utmost reaches of hell: priests who have left the ministry, religious who have adopted lay clothes, the reformers of the church's liturgy, communists, freemasons, modern theologians, heretical Christians, those who give or receive communion in the hand, women who wear sleeveless dresses, pornographers . . .

67

It is interesting to note that the revelations become increasingly vengeful as they proceed. In the earlier chapters, it is only God whose patience is wearing thin, and Christ is presented as shielding the world from the upraised arm of his angry Father. But as they proceed, Christ himself begins to share this wrath of God, and the merciful role has to be played by Mary:

> I will stay the arm of my Son, who is already impatient.

Will the time come when her patience too runs out, and men require yet a further human intermediary to protect them from the vengeance of heaven? And would not the whole process be totally alien to the New Testament, where Mary is venerated because she is the very image of Christ, and Christ is worshipped because he is the very image of God?

Clearly we need to be aware of the danger of too readily identifying our enemies with the enemies of God. Certain categories of people make us see red, and we naturally assume that they must make God see red too. This is of course naïve. All the same, the 'revelations' have at least this biblical backing, that some categories of people, whether they coincide with our pet hates or not, are there said to outrage God to the extent of meriting his wrath. It would be dishonest to draw attention to the texts about God's unswerving mercy, unconditional pardon and total love, without acknowledging the existence of these texts too. How are the two to be reconciled?

Perhaps they cannot. Perhaps there is no need to assume that all parts of Scripture are equal. Perhaps some of its insights are more valuable than others, and there are passages, in the New Testament as in the Old, which simply have to be acknowledged as not measuring up to the heights reached by the Bible as a whole. For its authors were not miraculously exempt from human prejudice, narrowmindedness and sheer ignorance, nor were they less liable than any other group of people to assume that God's preferences coincided with theirs. But texts of that kind are not to be confused with the whole. It is the totality of Scripture which is the word of God to men, and the totality assures men that God is not ultimately vengeful, but forgiving.

There is of course a danger in such an argument of picking and choosing those bits of the Bible which we find personally congenial. Yet even if it is granted that there is a gospel within the gospel, it would still be worthwhile to analyse more closely what the wrathful texts could mean. For even if an angry God is incompatible with a God who reveals himself as forgiving, the texts are vociferously aware that *something* is angry!

Is this anger a powerful way of expressing concern for those who get hurt when God is so unvengeful? An anguished cry of protest against injustice, and a wishful dream that the problem could be solved if only an angry God would intervene?

Or is it an expression of the seriousness of sin? A vivid awareness that selfishness and injustice and the exploitation of others are trivialized if they are thought not to matter? They matter so desperately that they would bring all hell about us were it not for God's love.

Or are the texts trying to say something about the seriousness of that love of God? For love is not simply tolerant, or permissive, or indifferent to the wellbeing of the beloved. On the contrary, love cares so desperately that the lover will go to death and beyond for the beloved. The Christian symbol of the cost of love is the Cross. Is it the vehemence of Calvary that lies at the heart of those vehement texts?

Or is it, finally, an awareness that such overwhelming love comes as a judgement on the world, not least on ourselves? A vivid consciousness of the poverty of our own love compared to the faithful and never-ending love of God? We speak of a situation being 'angry' when there is a total lack of harmony between what ought to be and what is. Is it this that people mean when they speak of an angry God?

There may be elements of all these in the texts which refer to the wrath of God. The term is a metaphor, an anthropomorphism, and is not to be taken literally. The reality behind the metaphor is not a God who will wreak vengeance on the sinner. On the contrary, the only response he will ever make is to love the sinner back into virtue, and his only demand on the sinner is to go and do likewise.

WHAT THE HELL?

Our understanding of God's wrath will, of course, affect our understanding of hell. One is the counterpart of the other. 'Hell' exists to receive the victims of God's 'wrath'. If one is a metaphor, does it follow that the other is too?

It is often thought that this question poses a problem only for readers of the Old Testament, as if there alone was God spoken of in terms of punishment, in contrast with the New Testament God of forgiveness. The truth is, of course, as we have already seen, that the theme of God's wrath figures just as strongly in the New Testament as in the Old. In fact, for sheer exuberance of expression, the New Testament far outshines the Old in developing the theme of punishment. Not only are sinners promised an eternity of frustration (the 'grinding of teeth' Matthew 13.42) and of torture (the 'undying fire' Mark 9.43), but the sentence is represented as being pronounced, with some relish, by Jesus himself (Matthew 13.41; 25.41). The Book of Revelation in particular, with its phantasmagoria of images, seems to take a positive delight in the punishment of the wicked, as they bleed, burn, writhe and suffocate to the applause of the saved (see especially chapters 14 and 19–20).

If one were to ask how such merciless images are to be reconciled with what we are told elsewhere of the love and mercy of God, the answer is again that they cannot. It is ridiculous to suggest that love has limits beyond which it cannot go, least of all in God. It is just as ridiculous to suggest, as preachers are wont to, that the dire warnings are spoken with infinitely loving compassion; no one reading the biblical texts can fail to note the loathing that lies behind them.

What, then, is to be done with the texts? Are they to be dismissed as an unfortunate lapse from the good taste of the rest of the Bible, a regrettable aberration on the part of the authors, not be be accorded the same authority as their more comfortable texts on God's love?

One ought, again, to be reluctant to solve the problem so neatly. It would be convenient to cut out of our Bible all texts which do not represent God as loving. But that love would be spineless. The hell-fire texts, like those about God's wrath, are presumably trying to say something about the seriousness of God's love, and the disastrous consequences for those who refuse to recognize that love or echo it in their own lives.

This does not mean that hell is to be taken literally as the punishment which God will inflict on such people. Them too God loves, and love simply is not love if it has a big stick laid by for emergencies. But people can punish themselves, and need to be told, urgently if necessary, that they fool themselves if they think that lack of love and betrayal of love will do anything other than diminish and ultimately destroy them.

> The New Testament statements about hell are not meant to supply information about a hereafter to satisfy curiosity and fantasy. They are meant to bring vividly before us here and now the absolute seriousness of God's claim and the urgency of conversion in the present life. This life is the emergency we have to face.
> (H. Küng, *Eternal Life?*, Fount 1985, p. 175)

Talk of hell cannot simply be dropped, therefore. Nor should it be diluted. It is meant to be taken seriously as an expression of what we have the frightening liberty of doing to ourselves. But it is not meant to be taken literally. There is not, in actual fact, a place or a state where certain people will be excluded for ever from the presence of God.

FOR EVER AND EVER

For the eternity of hell is also part of the picture language. It too needs to be taken seriously, for hell is what man's situation would inevitably and eternally be if God did not rescue him from his self-destructive urges. But at the heart of the Bible stands the good news that God not only has always cut the chains with which men would enslave themselves, but will continue to do so.

Men will always be free to call themselves God's enemies, but the enmity will be entirely of their own

making, not God's. On his side there can be only forgiveness and love. To believe in God means to believe
that such love will eventually overcome even the most
obdurate. Not by violence – for that would again be to
turn love into something other than love – but simply
because love is more powerful than the strongest resistance that can be put up against it. To yield to such a
power is not to lose one's freedom, but finally to find it.

It should have become obvious by now that hell-
language, like judgement-language, is much more about
the present than it is about the future. It describes not
what will happen to people after death, but what their
situation is today. For the choice between heaven and
hell, between self-fulfilment and self-destruction, lies
before us at every moment in our lives, and each decision we make is a turning point. Life is not morally
neutral. Right is right, and wrong is wrong, and the
issues which are now fudged will ultimately be made
clear. But to imagine that the only way in which this
can be done is by setting up a concentration camp in
the midst of an otherwise idyllic landscape[1] is to mis-
understand the power of a God whose love is the only
reason that flowers can grow, and people can forgive
each other.

Two contrasting news items recently caught my eye in
the paper. In Tehran a Muslim woman was witnessing
the execution of her son's murderer. As the rope was
being placed round his neck, she told the hangman to
stop. According to Islamic law, her forgiveness reprieved
the man. In America a Catholic bishop, much criticized
by his clergy, was sending his last letter to his friends
from his hospital bed. He wrote: 'I wish to let everyone

[1] The image is taken from J. A. T. Robinson's *In the End God* (SCM,
London, 1968).

know that I have forgiven my enemies. I can forget personal hurt because I am a Christian and a bishop. But God will not so forgive.' Which of the two actions was a truer reflection of God? Even Paul, who is not averse to talking of the wrath of God, was more deeply convinced that:

God has imprisoned all human beings in their own
    disobedience
only to show mercy to them all.
How rich and deep
are the wisdom and knowledge of God!

(Romans 11.32–33)

It is heartening to see how doggedly the English mystic, Julian of Norwich, clung to this basic insight, even when she was accused of heresy. She had no wish to challenge the church teaching of her time, that some people (Jews in particular) were consigned to eternal damnation. But she maintained repeatedly that such vindictive ideas formed no part of her visions, and insisted that it was precisely on the subject of sin that God kept assuring her, 'All will be well'. She was committed to the truth that reality is rooted in an unalloyed love which is simply incompatible with vengeance and wrath. She was convinced that, whatever the official theologians said, even the pain of remorse for sin could not last for ever, and that love (to be truly love) must ultimately triumph.

Synne is behovabil,
but al shal be wel
& al shal be wel
& al manner of thyng shal be wele.
(*Revelations of Divine Love*, ch. 27)

74

What, then, finally, is to happen to the devil? If there is no literal hell for him to preside over, is he to be made redundant and so dismissed?

It would not be easy to dismiss him. True, he plays little part in most of the Old Testament, but he had acquired (together with angels) such a firm foothold in the thinking of late Old Testament Judaism that he appears no less than 34 times in the pages of the New Testament under the title of 'Devil', and 33 more times as 'Satan'. He is mentioned not only in the ministry of Jesus as the source of the mental and nervous disorders which he healed, but also in his teaching, as the tempter, destroyer, murderer and liar who had gained control of a world which Jesus was determined to win back for God. Jesus even taught his disciples to conclude their prayer with a plea to be delivered from the Evil One (Matthew 6.13). The Book of Revelation, not unexpectedly, is particularly eloquent about the activity of this embodiment of evil, and of his eventual gory defeat.

These New Testament pages have had an enormous impact on people through the ages. Everyone has heard of the old lady who bowed her head in reverence whenever Satan was mentioned, and when asked why replied, 'It costs nothing to be polite'. At her age, she obviously thought it safest to hedge her bets. But then for many people, especially in the context of today's interest in the occult, Satan is a safer bet than God anyway. They are willing to remain sceptical about the existence of God, but about the existence of Satan they are left in no doubt whatever. The reality that this word stands for is somehow more tangible and more undeniable than the reality represented by the word 'God'.

It is important to try to pinpoint this reality. For while it might again be thought convenient to eliminate the New Testament's talk of the devil as 'sub-Christian', we would be the poorer were we to do so. We would lose not only the image, but all that the image stands for.

'God's in his heaven, all's right with the world' is one way of summing up the human situation. Some may find comfort in such a summary, but for most people it is so inadequate that it verges on the trivial. In their experience, all is not right with the world, and never has been. They are aware of the fact that their own faults can hardly ever be contained within the limits over which they have control – other people are willy nilly dragged into their wake. They are aware that, to add to the chaos, this is universally true. But there is more. They are aware of the existence of a vast and intricate network of evil for which no individual or group can be held responsible, and which is something even more than the sum total of men's sins. And they are aware that this sickness infects not only evil men but good men too: their power of doing harm will always far exceed their personal malice.

There is a corporate evil from which not even the innocent and the sheltered can escape. It is part of the price all must pay to be part of the human community. The newborn child begins to breathe it in with his first breath. Even Jesus could not escape its clutches (Mark 1.13 and parallels), and his second-in-command, for all his good will, found that he too was its unwitting agent (Mark 8.33).

To this radical evil men have given the name of Satan. The word means 'The Adversary'. The dramatic personification serves to underline the fact that its sheer intransigence, always thwarting men's best efforts and bedevilling their most idealistic aims, is felt as a kind of personal malevolence. Yet this evil power is not in fact embodied in some individual; the reality is something far more fearful.

This does not mean that talk of the devil should be dropped. The image continues to remind us of the superhuman forces in which the world is trapped. The 'demonic' in our world cannot be dealt with by the patient conversion of individuals from their personal faults. Man's predicament is not simply the result of men's individual sins, and it is naïve to act as if it is. The trouble lies deeper, and can only be dealt with by the creation of a new sort of humanity, where collective goodness begins to predominate over the satanic 'sin of the world'.

The New Testament proclaims that this is precisely what was achieved in the person of Jesus of Nazareth. In him, a new world was begun. In his life and self-giving death a new and liberating image of God had been revealed, to allow a new mankind to be born, animated by the same spirit of undying love. From now, in principle, men need no longer be prisoners of their past, for they knew that no power could resist the humanization offered to those who lived in the Spirit of Christ.

I watched Satan fall like lightning from heaven.

(Luke 10.18)

Now sentence is being passed on this world;
now the Prince of this world is to be driven out.
And when I am lifted up from the earth,
I shall draw all people to myself.   (John 12.31–32)

The Prince of this world is already condemned.

(John 16.11)

All authority in heaven and on earth has been given
to me.   (Matthew 28.18)

God has rescued us from the ruling force of darkness
and transferred us to the kingdom of the Son.
                                              (Colossians 1.13)

SUMMARY

It is time to summarize this lengthy chapter. If Scripture is in any real sense the word of God to men, then it
would seem that the themes of judgement, wrath, hell
and the devil are part of God's message to mankind.
They are the dark shadows thrown by the themes of
salvation, forgiveness, heaven and love. Without those
shadows, the positive themes would appear superficial.
They would lack a whole dimension, and could not be
seen in depth.

This does not mean that the dark themes qualify the
Bible's central theme, as if God were saving, loving,
forgiving and accepting up to a certain point. Judgement, wrath, hell and the devil are not threats held over
people's heads to ensure their good behaviour. On the
contrary, the good news is that at the deepest level
judgement has already been passed, the fearsome wrath
is not to descend, hell has been emptied and the devil
defeated. In the life and death of Jesus, God has
declared himself once and for all as the undeviating
forgiver of sins.

If the dark themes must continue to form part of the
Christian message, it is to draw men's attention to the
seriousness of human history. Evil continues to be a
dimension of that history, even in the lives of good
people and no one should imagine it is of little account.

It has the demonic power to reduce the world to the chaos out of which the Creator God originally rescued it.

Yet that creative act of God is the foundation of our hope. The love which overcame the primal darkness, which drew a living universe out of nothing and a living Christ out of the tomb, is stronger than all the powers of evil. The eternal lovelessness of hell may be a perfect image of what we can achieve by our own unaided efforts. But it cannot be a description of any sort of reality that will actually come to be, because it leaves out of reckoning the power of love.

6. The Coming of Christ

On the theme of the Coming of Christ, most of the Christians I know are agog with indifference. Each Advent the theme is put before them with considerable emphasis for a whole month. Scripture readings and sermons urge them to show some excitement over the imminent prospect of Christ's Coming. But they find it difficult to keep up the charade year after year.

Some of them feel guilty about this. If the early Christians breathed out their *Maranatha* – Come, Lord Jesus – with such fervour, ought this not to find an echo in their own prayer? If St Paul urged his readers to be faithful – not until death but – 'until Christ comes', ought they not to live their lives in the same perspective?

Yet who could blame them for their lack of enthusiasm? It was natural enough for the Christians of the year AD 50 to live in a fever-pitch of expectation for the coming of Christ; after all they were within shouting distance of the promise made to the disciples at his ascension that he would come again. But by the year 60 the theme had already worn so thin that it began to feature less and less in Paul's writings, until finally it disappeared from them altogether. What meaning can the theme possibly have for Christians living nineteen hundred years later still? For how long is one expected to continue responding to the cry 'Wolf'? Many Christians take their annual Advent preparation for the Coming of Christ about as seriously as the cartoon which shows a sandwich-board man standing at a snack bar. His bill-board proclaims 'The End of the World is Nigh', and he is saying, 'Coffee please – and make it instant!' More poignant still is the cartoon representing two ladies in earnest conversation, 'Is it true there is to be a Second Coming?' asks one. 'Yes,' replies the other, 'but not, I trust, in our lifetime.' The event which people once yearned for has become an event to dread.

COME, LORD JESUS

The same note of dread was sounded, as we saw in the last chapter, in the theme of Judgement. If Christ comes as judge, then the warmth with which he is welcomed will depend to a large extent on one's track record. The Old Testament prophets had already pointed out that the concept of the Day of the Lord contained a similar ambiguity. It was all very well to long for its coming so that the oppressors of God's people could receive their just deserts. But what if one's own faults were worse than theirs?

> You alone (Israel) have I intimately known of all the families of earth,
> that is why I shall punish you for all your wrong-doings. (Amos 3.2)

> Disaster for you who long for the Day of the Lord!
> What will the Day of the Lord mean for you?
> It will mean darkness, not light. (5.18)

The coming of God was not necessarily an unalloyed blessing. Indeed, it was such an ambivalent reality that people eventually spoke of a 'divine visitation', and meant punishment.

81

Yet the concept could have happier associations too. When Christians began to bestow on Jesus the Old Testament title of 'Lord' and to think, therefore, of the future Day of the Lord as the 'Day of the Lord Jesus Christ' (1 Corinthians 1.8, Philippians 1.6, 10), it was usually in terms of an ardently longed-for realization of the world's hopes. The supposition behind the phrase was that the first Coming of Christ had somehow fallen short of expectations. God's promises would not be completely fulfilled except by something far more decisive – a Coming of Christ in indisputable power and glory. He had come once in humility. He must come again escorted by angels on the clouds of heaven, to give full meaning to the great vision of Daniel which seems to have determined the title by which Jesus is most commonly known in the gospel pages – the Son of Man (Daniel 7.13-14).

This expectation of a future Coming of Christ features strongly in many pages of the New Testament, under a variety of titles: Advent, Appearing, Manifestation, Day of the Lord. It is the main theme of the notoriously obscure 'Eschatological Discourse' attributed to Jesus on the eve of his passion (Mark 13, Matthew 24-25, Luke 21). There it is given a sense of such imminence that the hearers are warned to maintain perpetual vigilance (Mark 13.33-37 and parallels). This sense of immediacy is echoed in a wide range of texts:

The time has come ... The night is nearly over, daylight is on the way.   (Romans 13.11–12)

The time has become limited ... This world as we know it is passing away.   (1 Corinthians 7.29–31)

As long as we have the opportunity let all our actions
be for the good of everybody.   (Galatians 6.10)

The Lord is near.   (Philippians 4.5)

Encourage each other; the more so as you see the Day
drawing near.   (Hebrews 10.25)

Only a little while now, a very little while,
for come he certainly will before too long.   (10.37)

Do not lose heart, because the Lord's Coming will be
soon.   (James 5.8)

The end of all things is near, so keep your minds calm
and sober.   (1 Peter 4.7)

'How much longer?' . . . They were told to be patient
a little longer.   (Revelation 6.10-11)

The Bride says, 'Come'. Let everyone who listens
answer, 'Come' . . . I am indeed coming soon'. 'Come,
Lord Jesus'.   (Revelation 22.17–20)

On the basis of these and similar texts, the second
Coming of Christ has become part of Christian faith
and hope. The basic Christian prayer, the 'Lord's
Prayer', yearns for a coming of God's Kingdom that still
lies in the future, and the Christian Creed ends with a
profession of faith that Christ 'will come again in glory'
to bring this about. One of the earliest liturgical formu-
las, translated in the last of the quotations above, is the
Aramaic *Marana tha* – 'Come, Lord' (so also in 1
Corinthians 16.22), and the first day of the week was

known from the beginning as the 'Lord's Day' to mark the fact that on that day Christians met to anticipate the 'Day of the Lord'.

THE PAROUSIA

One of the words with which the new Testament expresses this hope of a future Coming of Christ is Parousia. It means 'arrival' or 'presence', and was the technical word in the Roman Empire for the official royal visit of the provinces by the emperor. It occurs so frequently in Paul's letters to the Thessalonians that this correspondence forms a privileged commentary on this article of the Christian faith.

The Christians of Salonika clearly put the Parousia very high on their list of priorities, and they could not have inherited this scale of values from anyone other than Paul, who had converted them to Christianity about the year AD 50. Within months of his leaving to preach elsewhere, they were writing to ask what the delay was. They were horrified that some of the elder converts had died, and so had presumably missed out on the great victory celebrations. Paul wrote his first letter to the Thessalonians to comfort them in their distress.

Far from dampening their enthusiasm, the letter fired it to fever pitch. On receiving it, many in the Christian community panicked. The Parousia was obviously so imminent that they could go on the dole for the few weeks that still remained! Paul's second letter was a desperate attempt to restore sanity. In the nature of things, he wrote, there were certain events which had to precede the Parousia, and until there was clear evidence of these taking place, Salonika must stay calm.

One could have thought that by listing these events –

the Secret Rebellion, the Open Revolt, the Coming of the Rebel, the Obstacle (see 2 Thessalonians 2.1-15) – Paul had earned men's eternal gratitude for providing so much advance information on the Last Days. But on closer examination the details offer no information at all. They are all borrowed from an existing stock of images to which all the apocalyptic writers of his day turned – the gospel writers included – in order to speak of conflict and crisis, of world-shaking events, and of the emergence of a new world out of an old one.

Some people may be disappointed to discover that, in these precious pages of the New Testament which explicitly deal with the Parousia, we only have a generalized picture of the end of *a* world, not hard information on the end of *the* world. They may be even more disconcerted to discover that Paul, after so openly presuming that this event was near at hand, gradually realized his error and, as I mentioned earlier, quietly dropped the subject.

This was perhaps only to be expected, since there are limits beyond which 'a stone's throw' surpasses the reach even of a champion. But it should surprise no one to discover that, after an interval of a further nineteen hundred years, the Christian who still hopes for the Coming of Christ can only do so in the spirit of the Jews who, having waited a much longer time for their Messiah, tell the story of the *shtetl* elders who refused their Watchman for the Messiah the pay-rise he requested, 'because of the permanent nature of the employment'. Indeed, the present mayor of Jerusalem, Teddy Kollek, referring to his attempts to dissuade his fellow Jews from trying to offer Jewish worship at Muslim shrines, at least until the Messiah comes, added the characteristic remark, 'Of course, he may come next week, but that's a risk we all have to take.'

To say it once again, lest there be any misunderstanding, Paul gave up his earlier hope of a Parousia In Our Time. His later theme of a Coming of Christ in the present was not placed *alongside* the earlier theme of a future Coming, so that one should balance the other. One replaced the other. Yet in discarding his earlier belief about the future, he deepened his understanding of the present.

This needs explanation. Paul came to see that what lay at the very heart of a belief in the Parousia was a conviction, not about the unknown future, but about the experienced present. The belief was a commitment to what was ultimately true and ultimately decisive, and therefore, true and decisive now. All the hopes that the word Parousia expressed in terms of tomorrow were in fact available and realized today.

Whatever speculations one might make about the future, the Christian had to put his faith in a Christ who formed not simply the goal towards which he was straining, but the very hub around which his life revolved. For the distinctively Christian belief was that, in the life of Jesus of Nazareth, God had said all there was to be said to men. His life had finally disclosed the meaning and the purpose of the world's history. In him, therefore, history had achieved its end. However long the world may still continue, it would from then on be in its 'End Times' or 'Last Days'. The 'end' of the world could now be seen to consist not in its rejection or annihilation, but in its fulfilment. And this 'end' had begun in the life of Christ and in the birth of a community inspired by his Spirit.

In this light, the Coming of Christ can no longer be thought of as a future event. Christ comes, not when men's lives or the world's history draw to a close, but when men's lives are crossed and challenged by his in the midst of life and in the thick of history. The characteristically Christian belief is not in a 'second' coming, but in a constant coming of Christ into people's lives. In the deepest sense, the Coming of Christ is no longer a single datable event, but a reality of every day.

I have here briefly summarized a theme already mentioned a number of times in the preceding pages, particularly in the chapters on Resurrection and on Heaven. The pages of Paul there quoted make it clear that, in the last analysis, all his emphasis is on a resurrection which takes place now rather than later, a heaven which is to be celebrated on earth rather than in another world, and a life which is to be lived before death rather than after. Increasingly, in his correspondence with Corinth, Rome, Colossae and Ephesus, he speaks of all the hopes which he once focused on the Coming of Christ as being fulfilled in men's present embodiment of Christ in the church. There the new creation has already begun, and men's redemption, salvation and union with God are a present reality. There God's original plan for men is finally achieved, as Christ comes more and more fully into their daily lives.

NOW IS THE HOUR

We have returned to the subject of a 'realized eschatology', where the *eschata* or last things are no longer postponed to the future, but realized in the present. The New Testament's strongest spokesman for this viewpoint is St John, whose recurring phrases 'The hour is coming, *and now is*' (4.23; 5.25; 16.32; see also 2.4; 4.21; 5.28; 12.23, 27, 31; 13.1; 16.2, 25; 17.1) stands in

deliberate contrast with the futuristic outlook of
Matthew, who said:

> The Son of Man is coming at an hour you do not
> expect. (24.44)

> Stay awake, because you do not know either the day
> or the hour. (25.13)

According to John, Christians *do* know the hour. It
struck in the life of Jesus, when Daniel's Son of Man
was raised to eminence on a cross, and it continues to
strike in the life of each man as he recognizes that cross
as God's final revelation of himself.

Not that this is the only aspect of the early church's
eschatological hope that John reinterpreted. He recasts
each of its details so that the reader should know that
the Last Times are not in the future, but today.

The promised Day of the Lord will indeed dawn, but
it is the day when Jesus confronts men (8.56). And that
Day will indeed bring the expected Judgement, but this
is something that men willy-nilly pass on themselves in
their response to Jesus (3.18-19; 9.39; 12.31; 16.11).
Jesus will indeed return, and soon after his departure,
so that his disciples will see him again 'in a little while',
but this will not be anything different from their experience of being overwhelmed by the Spirit of Christ
pouring out of his dying body (14.18-19; 14.26-28;
16.16-22). The trumpet will indeed sound to rouse the
dead, but its sound is the voice of Jesus calling all men
to fullness of life (5.25; 11.43). The dead will indeed
arise to enter into eternal life, but this is something that
happens while people are still alive, when they recognize
Jesus himself as their resurrection (11.25), and realize
that eternal life consists in seeing God as he saw him

(3.36; 5.24; 6.47; 14.6; 17.3). All things will indeed culminate, as men always hoped they would, in a blaze of divine Glory, but that Glory already shone in the ministry of Jesus (1.14; 2.11; 11.40), and nowhere more brilliantly than in his death (7.39; 17.1).

Perhaps the most significant aspect of John's remodelling of eschatology is that he places most emphasis on it in his account of Jesus's last discourse before his passion. In the other gospels, this discourse was about the Coming of Christ in the future. For John, the Coming of Christ has no meaning if it is not understood in the present tense.

His reinterpretation is seen by some as a magnificent *faute de mieux*, a valiant attempt to salvage something of Jesus's teaching even when it had proved so wildly wrong on eschatology. It had become obvious that Jesus was not literally going to come again as soon as he promised, but there was no reason why he should not come again metaphorically!

But is it not more likely that, far from putting Jesus right, John was putting the other evangelists right? That what had proved wrong was not Jesus's message, but men's understanding of it? That what Jesus turned men's attention to was not a reward in an unverifiable future, but a fullness of life to be lived and tested by experience here and now?

Certainly the parables, which seem to constitute the most characteristic form of his teaching, all have about them a sense of crisis calling for men's urgent decision now. God's Kingdom comes as a challenge, like a Harvest ready for reaping, a Dragnet pulled into shore, a Treasure within reach, an Employee under notice of dismissal ... If men do not take action now, it could be too late. The fact that the evangelists later turned these parables into moral exhortations, or warnings about the future, should not be allowed to obscure their original sense of urgency. Christ 'comes' to inaugurate the Kingdom of God, not in the distant future, but now.

7. After Death, What?

Having mentioned more than once the guilt-feelings experienced by Christians on the topics explored in this book, and my assurance that these feelings are unwarranted, I now find myself with certain guilt-feelings of my own. Have I really rather cheated the reader so far? After all, my over-all title did promise to deal with the afterlife, and so far I haven't got anywhere near the topic. In all the areas we have touched on – Death, Resurrection, Heaven, Eternal Life, Judgement, Hell, the Coming of Christ – all I have said is that, to be true to the New Testament's sense of urgency, they must be seen as present realities, not future ones.

Does this mean that they are not future realities at all? Has that future totally evaporated? Has the emphasis on the here-and-now so taken over that there is no room left for what is yet-to-come? Is there in fact nothing beyond death? Or, at any rate, nothing that can be said? Has the Bible no information to offer about the future, only about the present? Are we condemned to be what St Paul calls the most pitiable of all men 'if our hope in Christ has been *for this life only*' (1 Corinthians 15.19)?

The reader will recognize these as questions which are being asked by more and more people in today's world, even by Christians, and even by Christians of the most traditional kind. People of a past age, with a far less scientific picture of the world they lived in, were not troubled by such questions. In their understanding of the world, the miraculous post-mortem resuscitation of corpses and their transfer to another world was quite within the bounds of possiblity. At least, it was no more unacceptable than men turning into werewolves or frogs into princes. But a universe which is seen as governed by rigid scientific laws allows very little room, if any, for a resurrection and a post-mortem existence of that kind. Is our understanding of the world we live in so different from that of the past that we can simply no longer cope with this article of our faith? Or, having reinterpreted it so that it no longer jars unbearably with our world-picture, is it still the same article of faith? Ought the modern Christian to come clean and say openly that he no longer believes in the resurrection of the dead and life everlasting?

MYSTERIES AND METAPHORS

To answer these uncomfortable questions we must recall some of the principles laid down in the opening chapter of this book.

The first of these is the need for a reverent agnosticism. We are dealing with the unknown. It is not that the mystery is too lofty for our earthbound minds, but simply that we have absolutely no information to go on. No one has returned, either from the grave or from the future, to give us any clue about the final destiny of the individual or of the world. This means that all thinking, writing, preaching or teaching on this subject is guesswork, and the honest man will say so. Even poets, whose guesswork is usually more inspired than that of theologians, have to admit that, for all their attempts to 'peep into glory', what lies beyond the dust is a mystery:

> Dear, beauteous Death! the jewel of the just,
> Shining nowhere, but in the dark;

What mysteries do lie beyond thy dust;
Could man outlook that mark!

And yet, as angels in some brighter dreams
Call to the soul, when man doth sleep:
So some strange thoughts transcend our wonted
    themes,
And into glory peep.

(Henry Vaughan)

If the obscurity of our subject demands that we exercise a certain agnosticism, its theological nature demands that we recognize the limitations of language. All theology, I said earlier, has to be expressed in metaphors: God cannot be spoken of literally. This does not mean that he cannot be spoken of at all. But it does mean that what we say about him is symbolic and inadequate.

Talk of life with God after death, therefore, is metaphorical, just as talk of life before birth would be. It is no more literally true to say that after death we continue to exist, than it would be to say that before birth we pre-existed. In literal fact, each individual existence has an end, just as it had a beginning. Eternal life is not literally something that succeeds historical life, taking over where our historical life stops. It is a metaphor or myth, just as reincarnation is a metaphor or myth. This does not mean it is nothing. The metaphor stands for something real. But it remains metaphor, and should not be presented as, or taken for, literal description.

PROJECTION

With no factual information to go on and only figurative language to use, what can the biblical authors say about the future? They can use their present experience to make an imaginary picture of the future, and project it on to a distant screen. After all they had to make a similar projection on to the past in order to talk about the imaginary beginnings.

On the 'first things' as on the 'last things', the biblical authors had no hard information. If they seem to describe the creation of the world and of man, and to tell the story of the first sin, it is only because they are reading their present experience of a world in God's hands, and of a mankind in rebellion against God, *back* into the past, and thereby professing their faith that the world and man are such by their very nature. The universe as they experience it has always been held in existence by God; and man as they know him has always struggled with God for the mastery of the world. The texts seem to be talking about the past. In reality they are talking about the present.

The biblical texts about the end things similarly seem to be talking about the future. In reality they are talking about the present in terms of the future. The authors had no information about what lay beyond death. What they did have was their present experience of God's love, and their certainty that it was not only stronger than death, but was constantly creating new life out of the nothingness of death.

Their conviction that this was not intermittently true, but persistently and eternally so, that it would still be true wherever one took one's stand, can only be conveyed by projecting that divine love on to the future. The vivid picture on the distant screen may create the illusion that that is where the reality exists. But the hoped-for (and feared-for) realities lie in the present. The purpose of life and the meaning of history are not determined by what will happen in an unknown future. The whole of it is here and now, within our experience, as fully as it ever will be. Freud was right when he said that heaven and hell were projections. He was wrong in thinking that what we projected was our irrational fantasies and fears; we project realities we have already experienced.

The point can perhaps be more clearly made by observing this process of projection actually at work. The Book of Revelation is a good example of what such a process throws on to the screen: image after brilliant image of the eventual defeat of evil, of the final salvation of the blessed and of the ultimate victory of God. But the 'slide' which is able to produce these dramatic pictures is far more existentially expressed in Paul's famous paean of praise:

> If God is for us, who can be against us? . . .
> Who can bring any accusation against those that God has chosen?
> When God grants saving justice who can condemn? . . .
> Can anything cut us off from the love of Christ? . . .
> For I am certain of this:
> neither death nor life, nor angels nor principalities,
> nothing already in existence and nothing still to come . . .
> will be able to come between us and the love of God, known to us in Christ Jesus our Lord.
>
> (Romans 8.31–39)

What lies at the centre of Paul's joy is not anything that has been revealed to him 'from the other side' but a present conviction. His certainty is not based on secrets disclosed to him but on his own experience: the love of God as he has witnessed it in Christ's life and in his own. It is this that makes him able to make a projection even beyond death. The worst that the future holds in store will still not be able to invalidate that one reality which he knows to be true. For insofar as he has already undergone many deaths, he has already had a taste of post-mortem life. If one were therefore to ask him, 'What will happen to you when you die?', he could only reply, 'I don't know, but God has never disappointed me yet. What I do know is that I shall still be in the hands of a God of love.'

GUESSWORK AND COMMAS

But *how* will Paul – or anyone else for that matter – still be in the hands of God? What form will this take? That is the question which we still seem to be dodging. In what sort of way will we live on after death, even if the word 'after' has to be put into inverted commas? And if a reply can only be given in the form of guesswork, it would still be preferable, many will feel, to have that rather than nothing at all.

Perhaps we can begin, at least, with something a little firmer than guesswork. There are all sorts of ways in which we know of, and have actual evidence of, people living on after death.

1. People live on, after death, in the memory of others. Let it be admitted straight away that this is a rather tenuous kind of afterlife, but it is not nothing. It should not be dismissed with the words 'mere', 'only', 'simply' or 'just'. The memory of those who have died continues to exercise a real influence,[1] and the 'mem-

---

[1] I came across a striking example of this in the reflections of a father whose child had died at the age of five: 'I think we owe it to Paul not to dwell entirely on the grief and sorrow. For neither grief, sorrow nor sadness were Paul's life style. Rather, he knew not grief, nor sorrow, nor sadness, nor suffering, but what he did know from the

orial service' continues to be a powerful way of bringing them again into the present, as those who celebrate the Christian eucharist ('Do this in *memory* of me') well know.

Yet memories do fade, and those who remember die themselves. Is there not some more lasting way in which the dead can live on?

2. People live on, after death, in the mark they have left on the world. If no stone can be moved without altering the whole environment, however minimally, what must be said of the imprint left by people? The world is a better or worse place because of the people who have made up its history. What they have achieved or destroyed is irreversible, and the good they have done is not – in spite of Shakespeare's pessimism – 'oft interred with their bones'; like the evil, it lives on after them.

To use a simple example, it is incontrovertible that the inventor of the alphabet still lives on in all who use the system of communication which he bequeathed to

---

time he was born until he died in my arms Sunday night, was love. And love he received. And love he gave – in abundance. He knew joy, fun, kindness and concern for everyone. Everyone Paul met was Paul's friend ... I believe the only hurt he knew was to see someone sad. And then he would say anything to make them happy.

'Therefore, I think a worse tragedy than Paul's death would be to measure his life span by the calendar. It's the normal thing to think it's all right to die at eighty but a tragedy to die at five. When we think this way it makes Paul's life look a waste. Paul's life was not a waste. But instead it reached a beauty, and a fullness, and a fruition in five short years that many, if not most, never reach. Paul knew the qualities that this life is all about. Especially what it should be about – love and concern.

'Therefore, it is our hope and prayer that while you share our sorrow, you will also help in some way to perpetuate, not just Paul's memory, but Paul's style. And in that way, Paul will live forever.' (Quoted in *Travelling to Freedom*, Liturgical Press Australia, 1971, p. 344).

the world. He certainly lives on in me as I write this, and in you as you read it. And if anyone still reads this book after I have died, I too will live on beyond the grave, at least in that respect.

3. People live on, after death, in their children and disciples. Many memorial cards carry the comforting words of St John Chrysostom, 'He whom we lose is no longer where he was before; he is now wherever we are'. There is no one who has not experienced this kind of afterlife lived by parents and teachers. The example they set, and even the expectations they had of us continue to exercise an influence long after they have died. Sons, daughters and pupils all inherit the characteristics – physical, mental, psychological – of those who brought them up, and often even their foibles. I recently caught myself doing the very thing about which years ago my family constantly teased my ageing father: I hopefully waved a burning match in the air before tossing it into the waste paper basket, and a moment later found myself confronting a sizeable fire. My father lives on in me in this way, and in many others.

It is a sobering thought that the values by which people live have all survived in this way. Were it not for this power of the dead past to live on into the present, each generation would have to begin afresh to create its own values. Some might think this highly desirable, but no one can dispute the fact that, at death, the dead do not simply cease to live.[2]

4. People live on, after death, in the wider community of which they formed a part. Individuals die,

[2] I wonder whether it would be possible to put a number of ghost stories under this heading. I mean those which deal with apparent trivialities like the one I read of recently, where 'a circle of light appeared in the gloomy room, and then vanished. "It's only my late husband", said the old lady. "He always comes when there's his

but the group which gave them life, and to which they too gave life, continues to live. This too must not be too easily dismissed as of little worth or value. After all, almost the whole of the Old Testament was lived on these terms. Abraham and all the other patriarchs, Moses and all the other religious leaders, David and all the other kings, Isaiah and all the other prophets and psalmists – these were content to die with no other reward than the knowledge that the community did not die, and that they lived on in its life.

It may be objected that this Old Testament philosophy of life has an unmistakable Marxist flavour, in its willingness to sacrifice the individual for the sake of the community. The truth is, of course, that the Marxist philosophy of life has an unmistakable Old Testament flavour: Marx was, after all, a Jew. But it should also be pointed out that the New Testament inherited this philosophy, for it too speaks of a Christ 'sacrificed' for the community. In fact this is what, in one sense, talk of his death and resurrection is about.

For the Christian belief is not that Jesus escaped death, or died only for a time, or avoided the fatal effects of death. Jesus died, as all men must, and his historical existence came to an end, as ours will. If he lives on, it is because there is a community which lives by all that he lived by. He is alive in those who are lived in by his Spirit. If people want to find him now, we do not direct them to a tomb. We can only point to the community which continues to embody him. 'Why look among the dead for someone who is alive?' (Luke 24.5).

---

favourite chocolate cake for tea, and I've made one today."' Is this a fumbling attempt to express a conviction that, in her loving relationship to him, her husband did in some sense live on? Certainly among primitive peoples there is a vivid consciousness of their ancestors living on into their lives, helping and guiding them even after death.

The same words, of course, are addressed to Christians too. The Christian who has died is now no longer to be found in the cemetery. He lives on in the Christian community, and the more deeply so as his life was one of love. For that love is larger than life, and stronger than death. It lives on beyond his death in those who love as he loved. The Orthodox Christians have a particularly vivid sense of their saints still standing beside them in love as they address themselves in love to God.

5. People live on, after death, in a new relationship with the whole world. Here we enter a more speculative area, where we scarcely have the words to express what needs to be said. But it is not unconnected with what has just been said about resurrection. For Christ's resurrection is misunderstood if it is thought of as something added to his death. 'The resurrection is not another event *after* his passion and death. [It] is the manifestation of what happened in the death' (K. Rahner, *Theological Investigations IV,* Darton, Longman and Todd, London, 1966, p. 128). His resurrection is not a second life he enters into, but simply the one life that he lived – now seen with the eyes of God, that is to say, now revealed for what it eternally is.

So too, the resurrection that Christians look forward to at death should not be envisaged as another life added on to this, like a large annexe into which they can now move. It is nothing other than this life seen finally as God sees it. To hope for resurrection is to hope that the life which one has lived may be raised before God, and acknowledged as helping towards the coming of his Kingdom into the whole of his creation.

For in dying, our relationship to God's creation takes on a new dimension. Instead of being safely insulated from the world around us, we enter into a deep communion with it. Instead of being isolated from our fellow creatures, we are finally at one with them. Instead of being embodied in one human individual, we are now embodied in all.

Some will feel uncomfortable with this kind of talk. It smacks of eastern mysticism and pantheistic philosophy, where the individual is 'swallowed up' in the whole. This they see as a diminishment rather than the fulfilment they long for. They are not sure that they can look forward to such a loss of individuality, where the distinctive 'I' is swamped by being

> Rolled round in earth's diurnal course,
> With rocks, and stones, and trees.
>> (W. Wordsworth, Lucy Poems)

But what if individuality, far from being a prize possession that must be safeguarded at all costs, is in fact an obstacle to our real fulfilment? What if our human personality, far from being diminished by being embodied in the human community, is thereby perfected? For our true self does not consist – as it seems to do for things – in an individual separateness, but in an ability to communicate. Personality in fact cannot exist except in terms of relationship with others. If that relationship extends to all, the personality is enriched, not impoverished.

I presume that this kind of thinking lies behind the Chinese story of the man who was given a glimpse of hell, and saw its inmates seated before a glorious banquet with chopsticks frustratingly six feet long. The inmates of heaven were in exactly the same situation, but they were feeding each other.

Someone who shares all that he has and all that he is with others, who is willing to lose his individual separateness in the body of mankind, does not thereby forfeit his personality. On the contrary, he finally achieves it. After all, is not God defined as love that loses itself by pouring itself out? And is it not man's calling to become like God?

6. People live on, after death, in the mind of God. Our language is inevitably becoming more and more rarefied, and may sound like pious jargon designed to obscure rather than clarify. But the phrase is meant to express the conviction that beyond that which comes to an end, there is not simply nothing. There is God. We do not die into nothingness. As a Jewish prayer puts it:

> We remember those who have departed,
> They have not died into the grave,
> but into the love and eternity of God.

In short, the believer is not someone who knows what lies beyond death. He is someone who is convinced that the God who had the first word (how, he does not know) will also have the last (how, he does not know).

Belief in the resurrection is not an appendage to belief in God; it is precisely the ... crucial test that belief in God has to face. Why? Because I cannot stop halfway with my absolute trust, but must follow the road consistently to its end. Because I entrust everything to this God, (including) what is absolutely final, victory over death. Because I have a reasonable confidence that the almighty Creator, who calls us from not-being into being, can also call us from death into life ... Because I am confident that he is the God of the end as well as the God of the beginning: Alpha and Omega. Anyone who believes this seriously of the eternally living God, who believes then also in God's eternal life, believes in his *own* – in man's – eternal life.

(H. Küng, ibid. p.142–3)

7. One of my teachers (who lives on in me) was very keen on the word 'comma' He had a horror of the full stop which seemed to suggest that the last word had been said, and always insisted that each of his lectures was to be understood as ending with a comma. Anyone reading these last paragraphs may say that they do not satisfy him as expressions of what the afterlife may have to offer. He demands more. I do too. That is why I end this section with a comma,

PRAYING FOR THE DEAD

In the light of all that has been discussed so far, what can finally be said about praying for the dead? If we can only fumble with words to express what might lie in store for those who die, how can we hope to say anything worthwhile on the effect our prayers may have on them?

Perhaps we could begin by asking ourselves what effect we expect our prayers to have on anything. Many prayers, when they are analysed, turn out to be little more than a request that two and two should not make four. There is a childish naïvety about such an approach to God which one would have expected adults to have grown out of, though many never do. We cannot pray to change the course of events miraculously, or to wheedle out of God something he would not otherwise have granted. Less still can we pray for special consideration to be shown to us and ours. It is monstrous to suggest that those who pray are divinely protected from the misfortunes that fall haphazard on, or are even divinely aimed at, those who do not pray.

What then do we expect to happen when we petition God, and what sort of cause and effect do we assume to be at work? It is easy enough to understand something of the process behind praying for oneself: if I ask to become more charitable, there is a good chance I might actually begin to do something about it. But how can this process operate for other people? How are my prayers supposed to influence Fred, especially when he is dead?

Many people imagine that praying for others works on a kind of Telstar principle, where requests beamed up from point A bounce off God on to point B. In such a convenient arrangement it would matter little whether point B was in this world or the next. I can't say that I am attracted by the image of God who miraculously rearranges his world under the stimulus of prayers of this kind. Perhaps the most we can do in the darkness that surrounds this question is to make another list of the effects that we do know prayer for others has:

1. Praying for the dead has an effect on ourselves. To pray for others at their death is to state that we too hope to be remembered when we are dead. This may do nothing much for the dead person, but it gives us the assurance we need of a community, and a relationship with others, which is not totally destroyed at death.

2. Praying for the dead strengthens our community with the dead. Those who have died into the past tense come back into the present and therefore, in a sense, live on, at least in our memory of them. This may be thought to be little enough, but it is not nothing. What sort of world would it be where the dead are never remembered? There indeed death would have had the last word.

3. Praying for the dead begins to restore the unity of mankind. Whatever we do in our lives either builds up the human community, or destroys it. Each of us has cause to blush at the amount of destruction we achieve in a lifetime. I was saying earlier that there is an irreversibility about this. Whatever has been done has changed things, and they can never again be as they were before. Yet we do not need to be fatalistic about this. Such is our God-given nature that the worst evils can draw the best out of us. Not that those who have died are in any position to let this happen. But those who pray for them are, and their prayer shows at least the beginnings of a willingness to restore the unity that their brothers have broken.

4. Praying for the dead assures us of God's love. Some people think that if they do not pray for them, the dead will not have their sins forgiven. This is blasphemy. God forgives all sinners, whether he is asked to or not. But in that case why pray for God to forgive them? Ask any lovers why thy continue to ask each other, 'Do you love me?' The words 'I love you' are not the reply to a question to which the answer could go either way. They are the reassurance without which love cannot grow. To ask God whether he forgives the dead is not to doubt his responses, but to hear again the marvellous words, 'Of course I do'.

Talk of purgatory, therefore, must not be taken literally. There is not in actual fact a place or a state where the dead are detained while they are purged of their sins. The word 'while' cannot apply to those whose time ends with death. This does not mean that we should abandon talk of purgatory. Like talk of hell it is not to be taken literally, but it should be taken seriously. It too is a projected picture of a present experience – that of the painful contrast between God's unswerving love and the meanness of our response. To speak of purgatory is not to offer information about another world. It is to put into a searing image our awareness that to become as human as God calls us to be is not the work of a moment. It is a long process, involving many painful transformations.

These transformations can take a whole lifetime. What it could possibly mean for such transformation to extend beyond our lifetime, we cannot conceive. Comma.

8. Conclusion

The story was told me by a Jew of the town which was given three days' warning of the arrival of a tidal wave. The priest called all the Catholics together and impressed on them the need to go to confession. The vicar gathered his congregation and told them to ask forgiveness from those they had wronged and to make amends. The rabbi met the Jewish community in the synagogue and told them, 'You have three days in which to learn to live under water.'

LIFE AFTER LIFE

The word survival means different things to different people. Christians think of surviving death – if they hope to survive at all – in another world. The Jews in the story were bold enough to think of surviving death in this world, the only one they knew of. What they were yearning for was not life after death, but life after life after life after life.

It seems to me important to present this positive aspect of what is known as the 'Old Testament mentality'. Too often the ignorance of an afterlife is presented only in negative terms, as if it could produce only frustration and despair. But in fact, in the case of the Old Testament, it produced a sensitivity to the passing world and an appreciation of life which is rarely found among those who have set all their hopes on another world.

Nor is this sense of cherishing the present confined to the Old Testament. The New Testament, as we have seen, inherited this love of life. It too had to plead ignorance of the future, and could only make an inference about it from the present. Its eschatology is no more than the picture language in which it expressed its present certainties. It is only able to speak of the ultimate triumph of God's love because it has already experienced that love, and knows it to be more powerful than death. Its images of the 'End' do not provide us with a map of the future, but with a criterion by which to judge the present.

It has been the theme of this book that this use of the future tense to explain the present is the clue to the New Testament's eschatology. When people ask, as my title asks, 'After death, what will really happen?' the New Testament's answer is to refer them back to their present experience. If they have not seen death there, and judgement, and hell, and resurrection, and eternal life, then heaven alone knows how they will ever understand what is supposed to lie in the future. They would have nothing to relate that new experience to. Can a person who has never known love in any form have any idea of the God who is defined as love?

OVER-EMPHASIS

Yet that must not be my only conclusion. It is true that an escapist preoccupation with the future, typical of a certain kind of Christianity, needs to be corrected by the New Testament's stress on the present, and that is what this book has tried to do. But paradoxically, that Christian neglect of the present has been accompanied by an over-emphasis on the present in another direction, and this too has led to a lack of balance.

I am referring to the absolute and exclusive terms in

which Christianity has often been presented by Christians. If Jesus is God's Word, as Christians claim, in whom all that God has to say to mankind has been said; if in him all God's plans and promises were definitively fulfilled; if he is the long-awaited Messiah ushering in the messianic times, so that these are a present reality and not simply a future hope; if the Kingdom of God has come in the community which lives in his name and in his Spirit – then what *raison d'être* could there possibly be for any other religion? To be faithful to such a Christ, can Christianity do anything other than condemn those who do not acknowledge him as the Messiah? Can it conceive of its mission in any other terms than the conversion of others with a view to making Christianity co-extensive with mankind? Must it not proclaim that all non-Christians are in error, even if inculpably so, and demand that they renounce their errors, since outside the Christian church there can be no salvation?

There is no question that Christianity has in the past been preached in these exclusive terms, and in some places it still is. There is also no question that the world in which we live will no longer tolerate such intolerance. Nor do I mean simply the non-Christian world; over the years many Christians have themselves become increasingly embarrassed by the intransigence of the church's 'official line', and have wondered when the officials would see the light. In recent years ecumenism, once anathematized as the work of the devil, has been cautiously welcomed as the work of the Holy Spirit. Since that time, the church's mission can no longer be defined simply in terms of conversion; its relationship with others is today seen as a dialogue, in which the church hopes to learn and not to teach, certainly not to convert.

What then is to become of all the fine words in the

preceding chapters about a realized eschatology, about a Christ in whom history has achieved its purpose, and about a Christianity which is called to acknowledge that it has rceived God's final revelation of himself? What is to happen to the finality of Jesus's message?

PRESENT AND FUTURE

It is clear that Jesus's original preaching was expressed in terms of the present, the here and now. His message was not, 'The Kingdom is coming soon' but 'The Kingdom of God is in your midst'. The finality of such words is unmistakable. Jesus regarded his word and work as bringing God's plans to a crisis point. He spoke with a sense of urgency which demanded decision and commitment. Through his ministry the last times had come upon men and eternal choices had to be made. His teaching took up the future-oriented hopes of his contemporaries and transposed them all into the present: judgement is not in some distant future but now; the gift of God's Spirit is not tomorrow but today; eternal life and the Kingdom of God are realities to be lived not in an afterlife but in the present.

Yet in spite of the urgency of this message, Jesus was reluctant – to say the least – to assume the title of Messiah when it was offered him. This is clear from a whole number of gospel passages. He never for a moment claimed that in his ministry the age-old expectations of his people were fulfilled. Indeed any fool could see that they were not. He would immediately have taken sides with the rabbi to whom a Christian theologian was trying to prove that the messianic times had come; the rabbi simply looked out of the window and remarked, 'I see there's a cat and a dog fighting out there'. While we continue to exist in the disharmony which allows cat to fight dog, or the lamb to hesitate before lying down with the lion, it is a little premature to talk about Kingdom Come.

In what sense, then, was Jesus's message so final? Why, in that case, did he put so much emphasis on the present moment? What was so new about his teaching that demanded such urgent commitment?

Nothing, surely, except the reapplication of a timeless insight into the ways of God with men. He did not claim to preach a strange new doctrine, only to say in a new way what God has always been trying to din into people: that he is a God who summons men out of death, not once but many times, and again and again opens for them the door to life. The ultimate choices are therefore always urgently upon us, and we experience the mystery of life and death in each 'now'.

This means that the problems of the world we live in cannot be shrugged off into another world – indeed the prophets never envisaged such a world. It is in our world, the only world we know, that the Kingdom has to be made into a reality, and the only time for doing that is now. Salvation is constantly near, because it is constantly in the hands of men to make it or mar it. The question men must ask themselves is not *when* the creation of a new age will be brought about, but *how.* Their eyes must be focused not on the horizon but on their own heart.

What the whole of Judaism had been about, from the very beginning, was the radical seriousness of the life that men live in God's world. As a true Jew, Jesus preached nothing different. As a successor of the prophets, he wanted to do nothing other than see the world of men with the eyes of God. Hence the urgency, and in a sense the finality, of his message.

But it should be clear by now that this finality is no different from that of the message preached by the prophets. The salvation that is offered to people is always today, not tomorrow. Indeed, to postpone salvation to tomorrow is to risk missing it altogether. To indulge in fantasies about the future is very effectively to avoid the transformation with which we are challenged in the present.

But that is far from saying that this transformation has already been achieved, or that Christianity is to be identified with Kingdom Come. A child can see that it is not, and Jesus said that it should know (Mark 10.13). The Christian cannot claim that the new creation is already upon us without recognizing that tomorrow can be different from today, and thereby accepting the responsibility to bring that about, not least in the church itself. The gospel is concerned with the present vision which must inspire the Christian's life, but out of that vision he must also build the future, or there will be no future.

THE ONCE AND FUTURE CHRIST

In the light of these last remarks, Christians should perhaps examine carefully what they mean when they claim that Jesus *is* the Christ. In one sense, of course, they cannot do other than acknowledge him as God's promised Messiah, in spite of Jesus's own ambiguous attitude to the title. For they know no other person who so clearly expresses what God has always planned man to become. If they did, it is him they would have to follow rather than Jesus. He is for Christians the Word in which God reveals himself, and the Way on which men may reach God. To live as he lived is to achieve the purpose of life.

112

Yet, in another sense, Christians cannot absolutize these claims, or seek to impose them on others. If the messianic times have not yet arrived in their fullness, then the Messiah has also not yet arrived in his fullness. If the Kingdom of God has still to be built, and cannot yet be said to have come, then there is a sense in which Jesus is not yet 'the Christ', and has yet to come. Christians, like non-Christians, need to find the redemption of the world not only in the past, but also in the future.

How then should Christians speak of Jesus? Jesus is the model of what man is called to be. He reveals the destiny of the whole human race. He is the promise and guarantee of what human life can be like. He embodies the radical transformation which is offered to all people, not in some miraculous future, but every day. Yet insofar as that transformation remains incomplete, the Christian's eschatology, like that of everyone else, has to be called 'unrealized'.

The balance between the 'realized' and the 'unrealized', between the 'already' and the 'not yet', is a delicate one. We rarely hit it exactly right. We overbalance to one side when we despair of daily life and take flight into a future where everything will hopefully be put right; but of course the future can only be built in the present. We overbalance to the other side when we complacently imagine that we have already arrived in the perfect future and that there is nothing more to work for, least of all in ourselves; but of course Christianity is as much in need of an ongoing critique as any other institution.

Christianity is always infinitely more than the promise of pie in the sky when we die, though that is how it appears to most non-Christians, and to many Christians too. But it is also always infinitely less than Kingdom Come. Jesus *is* the Christ insofar as he anticipates the glory of the end days. He *will be* the Christ when all men have entered into the glory which he pre-figured.

9. Postscript

I append here, as in other books in this series, the text of a number of talks which I was asked to give by the BBC. In this instance they are five short commentaries on the book of Ecclesiastes, whose questioning tone seemed to me to be in keeping with the kind of questioning I have myself adopted in this book. Though the author claimed to be even more in the dark on the subject of the afterlife than we are, we can still be grateful for the light shed by his perceptive comments.

The talks were preceded by a 'thought' which drew attention to its main point. The translation of the text of Ecclesiastes is by Peter De Rosa.

WHAT'S IT ALL ABOUT?

Even dissatisfaction with life can be a way of knowing God.

> Vanity of vanities! It seems to me
> No fool could doubt that all is vanity.
> The beautiful itself is wearisome:
> All the risings and the settings of the sun,
> The circuits of the winds from north to south
> And all streams ending in the sea's large mouth.
> There's nothing to relieve the monotony:
> What is . . . what was . . . is what will always be.

The book of Ecclesiastes. His words, some people may feel, provide a very apt commentary on a Monday morning, as the weekly grind starts all over again. Others may think these words rather strange on a religious programme, even if they are from the Bible, Well, perhaps they are. And so are the next words:

> Wine, women, song – I gave them all a try.
> If I must go, what better way to die!
> I selected for my board the oldest wines
> And for my bed the youngest . . . concubines.
>
> I splashed my life with juiciest delights,
> With long and drowsy days and riotous nights.
> Pleasure of such intensity is pain,
> Yet when it passed I looked for it again.
> My eyes changed course as often as a fly;
> Nothing they settled on could satisfy.

What a world-weariness is there! And how accurately our author has caught the disillusion of our affluent society which, like him, has tried everything, and is still left feeling empty and unfulfilled.

But surely, we'll say, he's searching in the wrong place for fulfilment. What about contemplation and reflection on the meaning of life? Surely that's where the really wise man would look. But Ecclesiastes has tried that too:

> Wisdom itself I now began to hate;
> It is too fragmentary, it comes too late.
> When wisdom is your friend, the world's your foe,
> The more you know, the more your sorrows grow.
> I was gifted, people said, with common sense,
> So I decided not to spare expense:
> I would discover where true wisdom lies.
> A man has a right to know before he dies.

I tested wisdom and folly. Wisdom won.
The fool would put a blindfold on the sun.
At least the wise man's eyes are in his head.
Yet – in a hundred years they'll both be dead.

A shattering thought. This time next century, all of us, dead. If you like, the wise man is better off than the fool, who doesn't know whether he's coming or going. But if it all ends in death, what's the use? So?

So under the sun I toil every day;
At nights this brutal thought won't go away;
No matter whether I've been good or sinned,
All's vanity, a wild chase of the wind.

The book of Ecclesiastes is not the most optimistic book in the Bible. Even its first readers found some of its comments hard to take, and insisted that there are things which make life worthwhile: hard work, pleasure, generosity, love ... And Ecclesiastes simply replied, in all honesty, 'They don't satisfy me. They don't fill the void in my heart. My longings and yearnings are always greater than anything you, or anyone, can think of.'

And isn't that worth saying? It seems to me a more worthwhile comment on life than the glib complacency which thinks that life is an open book, and that any wise man – or any fool – can tell you what it's all about.

When we are bewildered and disillusioned, when we keep stretching out our hands for something greater (a bigger house, a better job, hoping that might satisfy us, until we've got it), isn't it God we're really searching for? Not the God who's the neat solution to a problem in arithmetic – we'll encourage atheism with a God like

that. But the God who is the mystery we have to keep
on and on searching for.

THE ABSURDITY OF LIFE

*If there is a God, it's believers who are going to find him
most puzzling.*

> Each of the seasons has its fruit to bring;
> Under heaven there's a time for everything:
> A time for being born, a time to die;
> A time to tell the truth, a time to lie;
> A time to whisper and a time to shout;
> A time to eat, a time to go without;
> A time to ravage, a time to mend a fence;
> A time for sex, a time for abstinence;
> A time to laugh, a time to shed a tear;
> A time to go, a time to reappear;
> A time for stillness, a time for gales to blow;
> A time for spring, a time for winter's snow;
> A time to open, a time to close the gate;
> A time for loving and a time for hate;
> A time for peace, a time to go to war;
> A time to ask what all the heartache's for.

Everyone knows those lines of Ecclesiastes. Most people
find them rather uplifting: 'There's a time for everything, isn't that marvellous!'

I'm sorry to disappoint them. The lines are intended,
like the rest of Ecclesiastes, to be deflating. There's a
time for everything: that really is terrifying. There's
nothing – living, loving or laughing – which can't be
swallowed up by its opposite. Nothing is permanent,
least of all ourselves:

Sharp time takes everybody unawares.
As fish are caught in nets and birds in snares
Time nets and snares us all, both you and me;
We wriggle and moan, but still we can't break free.

Is there anyone who hasn't experienced this relent-
lessness of life, this feeling that we're no more than cogs
in a machine? And there are even darker moments,
when life feels less like an ordered machine, more like a
game, where everyone's the loser:

Is this our life a thing to shout about?
Isn't it upside-down and inside-out?
Absurdity! A baby dies at birth;
A speck within an eye blots out the earth;
A gust of wind upon a tree may blow
And smash what took a century to grow.
Vanity of vanities! It seems to me
No fool could doubt that all is vanity.

The absurdity of life! How familiar these thoughts
would be to many of our modern authors and play-
wrights. What a surprise to find them in a book which
Jews and Christians venerate as the Word of God.

And if you ask, 'What has this to do with religion? All
it does is depress me!' I have to answer that if religion's
only response to the anguish in people's lives is to
smooth it over, or to pretend it isn't there, then indeed
religion has become what its critics say it is, an opium,
a drug which deadens our sense of what's really going
on.

I recently heard a sermon which was comparing the
theme songs from two old films, and asking which
expressed better a truly religious attitude, Rita
Hayworth's *Bewitched, Bothered and Bewildered*, or

Gene Kelly's *Singin' in the Rain*. The preacher chose the second. He said the real believer makes light of his troubles. Well! That's hardly how I understand the struggles and anguish of men of faith like Abraham, or Moses, or Jeremiah. Less still of a man like Jesus. Least of all on Calvary.

They found their life, and their death, bewildering, if you like absurd. What enabled them to cope was not the thought that life is just a puddle to be danced through, but the conviction that, bewildering as it is, God still stands at the heart of it.

Is the husband whose wife has just died of cancer, or the mother whose child has died at birth, or the woman whose marriage has broken down – singing in the rain?

All of us at some time have to face this dilemma: in an impermanent life, how can we find something permanent? And the rock to base our lives on won't necessarily be a set of neat and tidy answers to crucifying questions. I'm convinced that a man isn't a real believer if he's always entirely happy with God, and has never been puzzled by his arrangements for his world. But I'm also sure that the answer lies in a continued search, and deeper prayer. Would we be searching for God if we hadn't already somehow found him?

LOVE AND DEATH

Why did God make me? To be happy with him in this life.

Vanity of vanities! It seems to me
No fool could doubt that all is vanity.
Can man, this rational animal, be sane
With eternity lodged in his tiny brain,
Immortal longings crowding in a shell,

120

Haunted by hopes of heaven, fears of hell?
God made him. Why? Ask God, I cannot tell.

What is life all about? Why did God bother to make us?
What's it all for? Poor Ecclesiastes, who's set himself
such limitless questions, is afraid they're going to burst
his head. Can he find a safety valve by imagining
another life where all these questions will be answered?

> Which one of us is able to decide
> If there is life or death the other side?
> Fishes can't fly, nor birds swim in the sea;
> Man's not in his element with mystery.

It would be easy, wouldn't it, to shuffle off all our
problems by putting them on a shelf labelled 'To Be
Solved Later'? But Ecclesiastes no sooner toys with the
idea of an afterlife than he rejects it, as all his contemporaries did. Whether there is an afterlife or not, it
doesn't solve the present problem. So how does he cope?

> Our guiding principle is God knows best.
> This splendid misery is but God's test
> To prove to man he's nothing but a beast,
> Animal dough with animal breath for yeast.
> When this strange yeast escapes he knows he must
> Be what he was: black flour, common dust.
> And yet I've found man has the curious whim
> That the breath is special that pulsates in him.
> Religion tries to tell him when he dies
> The breath of beast goes down, his own will rise.
> Do beasts have priests and console themselves with
>   lies?

121

That is strong, isn't it? To us it sounds almost blasphemous, this dismissing of our religious beliefs as a projection of our fantasies and fears. Why is Ecclesiastes so angry about the suggestion, so strange and new to him, that there may be a life after death? Because for him it confuses the issue.

The traditional teaching held that good people are rewarded by God with happiness, and that bad people are punished. Ecclesiastes has said all along that there's simply no evidence for this in our existence. If you now say, 'Well, it may not happen in the here-and-now, but it will happen in the hereafter', Ecclesiastes can only reply, 'A set of false teeth tomorrow is no compensation for having my teeth knocked out today!

'Besides, what sort of God does that leave you with? A God whom you serve only because you hope for his reward, or fear his punishment? That sort of God is too small for me. I need a God whom I can serve for himself, however little I understand his ways, even if there's nothing in it for me later. Whatever you may say about life hereafter, I want a God whom I can live for now, today.'

> Better to be alive than dead. Here's why:
> The living know that they are going to die;
> At least they see the Nothing that's ahead.
> The dead do not suspect that they are dead.
> So get your dusters out as I pass by;
> You'll soon have need of them, for what am I?
> An old man musing at a window ledge,
> A ripple trembling on the water's edge,
> The last gleam of a pallid, sunken sun.
> While you have the energy, young men, have fun.

Does that last piece of advice sound cynical? It's not meant to be. It's meant to be a humorous but honest acknowledgement that life has its good moments. These good moments will never satisfy our yearning, because that is infinite. But that's no reason for renouncing them, rather for accepting them gratefully. We don't please God by being deliberately miserable now. If our holy talk about the next world makes us forget that the real problem is how to live in this world, how, in Christ's words, to be blessed today, hasn't it been worthwhile reading Ecclesiastes?

THE WRETCHEDNESS OF LIFE

Even Christ ended his days saying, 'God, why have you abandoned me?'

> Tears! In my life I've seen too many tears
> Flooding the well-worn runnels of the years.
> Tears of the uncomforted, the most oppressed;
> Of gentle people they were the gentlest.
> The smiling oppressor very rarely knows
> That thorns of his have pierced the quiet rose.
> Happier the dead than the bereaved,
> The still-born than the unborn, I believed.
> Happiest of all the unconceived.

I'm looking at a picture of a wartime refugee. She's staring straight into the camera, with tears flooding down a face already furrowed by years of hardship. These aren't the first tears she's shed. Nor would it be difficult to match this picture with the tears each of us has known.

> Poor man, poor man! So full of empty dreams,
> Of mad, mad longings and of futile schemes,

123

He crawls out of the womb where he lay curled,
A maggot in the apple of the world.
Head first he comes, in time feet first he goes
And in between what wretchedness he knows.

How pitiful a thing our life is. And how vulnerable. Think of the care with which we have to protect the soft skull of a newborn baby. Perhaps life wouldn't be so bad if those who got hurt most deserved it most. But often it's exactly the other way round:

The wicked I've seen interred with pomp and state,
God's holiest place they used to desecrate,
Yet preachers of their innocence show proof!
Their panegyrics are obituaries of truth!
The virtuous man is bound to feel betrayed
When sentence on such sinners is delayed.
I hope that God, wherever he is, has heard:
Evil's encouraged when punishment's deferred.
Love God, all will be well, though sinner's crimes
Increase a hundred or a thousand times.
God chastens those who keep on doing wrong;
The shadow of their days will not grow long.
This is my faith; it isn't very strong.

Here we're at the very heart of what Ecclesiastes has to say: 'This is my faith – it isn't very strong.' What are we going to do when a presumably just and loving God does nothing to even out the manifest injustices going on under his very nose – innocent people suffering, dishonest people being preferred to men of integrity? Shall we pretend that life is not unjust and tragic? I can't imagine God likes being defended by lies and pious phrases.

Well then, shall we hope that God will eventually

intervene to turn the tables? But there's no evidence that he's ever done so, or that he's that sort of God.

All right, then, shall we simply accept life's injustices with humble resignation? But that would be equivalent to saying God doesn't care. To cry out with anger against the situation, yes against God himself, to protest loudly, 'This should not be so', that's at least to acknowledge it does concern God. And that's already a prayer.

And so Ecclesiastes hovers on the knife edge. He can't bring himself to deny that God is just. But neither can he bring himself to assert it with any great conviction. And perhaps here we are close to what faith is – a constant anguished searching for the hidden God.

We have to accept the fact that God is indeed silent, and in one sense absent, because like a trusting Father he loves us enough to let us be, without interfering. But what we sometimes feel as an absence may be his closest possible presence, in love. Certainly that's how he was present to Jesus, on his cross.

OLD AGE

Faith isn't possible without some sort of doubt.

Young man, remember God while you're still young,
Remember him before the dark days come.

We've reached the last chapter of Ecclesiastes. He's been searching and searching for the face of the hidden God. And here he's searching the hardest as he reflects on old age, the dark days as he calls them.

The religious people of his time said they were the brightest days. A ripe old age was proof of a life well spent, and God's reward for a life of virtue. Ecclesiastes has his doubts. Better serve the God you know while you're young, while you still have your wits about you.

I don't know any description of old age which surpasses the picture Ecclesiastes paints: the indignity which old age brings to all our faculties – arms, back, legs, teeth, eyes, ears, and the hair turning white like blossom on a tree:

Don't wait until the sturdy guards are bowed
And erstwhile straight-backed, mighty men are cowed,
When all the grinders cease for they are few
And the eyes of window-peerers are wet with dew
From a night out of which no new sun ever rose.
Don't wait until some unseen hand shall close
The door upon the bright and crowded street
With its sounds of grinding and of scurrying feet.
Don't wait until the twittering of a bird
Can make you jump like sudden thunder heard.
I tell the young, I tell them what I see.
I see white blossom on the almond tree,
Old grasshopper that drags himself along
Dead fires in dead hearts where they belong.

Only an old man could have written those lines, with their painful awareness of diminishing strength and failing faculties. 'I tell the young, I tell them what I see.' These indignities are what anyone can see in old people's homes, in psychiatric clinics, in the wards of terminal patients. Shall we put on rose-coloured spectacles when we describe the last phase of man's journey to his everlasting home? Or shall we simply tell what we see?

Man there I see with mourners on the road;
I see him going to his abode
Where he will live uncaring endlessly.
My son, my son, these are the things I see.
Soon, soon, the snapping of the silver thread,
Soon breaks the golden lamp by which you've read;
The pitcher at the fountain where it fell
And soon the turning wheel beside the well.
You too, and soon, like everything will break.
The God who gives decidedly will take.
Your dust you'll mix with dust within the grave,
Your spirit render to the God who gave.
Vanity of vanities! It seems to me
No fool could doubt that all is vanity.

Those are probably the most poignant lines in the whole of this remarkable book. Even the old age and the retirement which so many people look forward to, to give them some respite from the rat race, even that only opens on to an emptiness darker than all the rest. Ecclesiastes doesn't say this with bitterness, but with infinite compassion and pity. Life is not as it's painted in the glossy brochures and the coloured magazines. There are aspects of it which can shatter anyone sensitive enough to look beneath the surface of things. Poor man, poor man.

How did it happen, I have to ask myself, that people ever accepted this book which questioned the meaning of life so disturbingly and so ruthlessly? Why didn't they condemn Ecclesiastes as a heretic for daring to criticize the answers people had given in the past to human misery?

Perhaps because they saw that his questioning faith was more worthwhile than the faith which never asks questions. After all, who is the true believer, the man who simply repeats the answers his forefathers have handed on to him because they comfort him, or this 'disbeliever' who broke through to the realization that we have to put our faith not in answers, but in God.